YORK NOTE

General Editors: Professor ,
of Stirling) & Professor Suh
University of Beirut)

Bruce Dawe

SELECTED POEMS

Notes by K. L. Goodwin
MA DIP ED (SYDNEY) D PHIL (OXFORD)
Professor of English, University of Queensland

LONGMAN
YORK PRESS

YORK PRESS
Immeuble Esseily, Place Riad Solh, Beirut.

LONGMAN GROUP UK LIMITED
Longman House, Burnt Mill, Harlow,
Essex CM20 2JE, England
Associated companies, branches and representatives
throughout the world

© Librairie du Liban 1984

All rights reserved; no part of this publication may be
reproduced, stored in a retrieval system, or transmitted
in any form or by any means, electronic, mechanical,
photocopying, recording, or otherwise, without
the prior written permission of the copyright owner.

First published 1984
Third impression 1990

ISBN 0-582-79221-5

Produced by Longman Group (FE) Ltd.
Printed in Hong Kong

Contents

Part 1: Introduction *page* 5
    Australian poetry in context   5
    Dawe's special place in Australian poetry   8
    Dawe's life   9
    Influences   16
    A note on the text   17

Part 2: Summaries   18
    A general summary of *Sometimes Gladness*   18
    Detailed summaries of selected poems   19

Part 3: Commentary   56
    Major qualities   56
    Australian in language   56
    View of life   57
    A satirical writer rather than a writer of satires?   58
    The upside-down view   59
    Mock-heroic and mock-mundane   60
    An all-embracing view   61
    Revitalisation of ordinary language   62
    Subjects   62
    Political satire   63
    Elegiac tone   63
    Popularity   64
    Humour   65
    Criticisms   65
    Conclusion   66

Part 4: Hints for study 67
  General approach 67
  Some areas for study 68
  Sepcimen answers 71
Part 5: Suggestions for further reading 76
The author of these notes 78

Part 1
Introduction

Australian poetry in context

The spread of English as a language of conquest, colonisation, trade, and education has had some startling effects unintended by the British government and the officials of the former British Empire. In India, the West Indies, and Nigeria, for instance, the English language became a means of unification for liberation movements that were successful in negotiating or seizing freedom from their English-speaking overlords. In such countries English was an imposed language, at first resented by the subject peoples but later used towards their own ends.

Much of the British Empire was based on exploitation, either in the form of plantations (using indigenous or imported slave labour) or as the administrative exploitation of raw materials and local manufactures. But in some countries (such as Canada and New Zealand) the purpose of the Empire was colonisation, resulting in the pushing aside of the indigenous peoples and the establishment of self-sufficient rural industries. The colonists from Britain brought the English language and its cultural heritage with them. They were not particularly concerned to impose the language or heritage on the people they had displaced; they tended to despise or ignore them.

In Australia, the pattern of colonisation differed in two major aspects from what happened in Canada and New Zealand. First the indigenous people, the Australian Aborigines, were more brutally treated than in the other colonies. They were almost entirely dispossessed of their land and in many parts of the country were completely wiped out. Secondly, the colonists brought with them a plentiful supply of slave labour. Unlike the slave labour in the West Indies, however, it was not made up of people from a different part of the world (West Africa, for example). It consisted of subject members of the colonising nation itself. They were convicts, mostly English and Irish, who had been found guilty by English courts of various crimes (many of them very minor) and sentenced to a period of transportation (commonly seven or fourteen years) to Australia. Once in Australia, most of them were used for government projects such as the collecting or quarrying of lime, the building of ports and roads, the construction of public buildings, and the provision of food. Some convicts were later assigned to free settlers and military officers and were used by them as unpaid labour to grow crops and look after sheep and cattle.

The British settlement of Australia began at Sydney (the 'Botany Bay' colony) in 1788. The poetry that the convicts, marines, and free settlers brought with them ranged from later eighteenth-century cultured poetry (such as that of Edward Young (1683–1765), William Collins (1721–59), Thomas Gray (1716–71), Samuel Johnson (1709–84) and Oliver Goldsmith (1730–74)) to the work songs and insurrectionary ballads of the Irish convicts. From the beginning, white Australian society was split into the rulers and the ruled. The officers of the marines and the army tended to support, with the free settlers, the continuation of respectable English culture. The convicts, with the rank-and-file marines and soldiers, had a popular, orally transmitted culture, including work songs, protest songs and bawdy songs with a bitter, black humour.

Eventually, of course, all the convicts had served their sentences and become free, and in time the colony was able to resist the attempts of the British government to send further convicts. Theoretically all the white people in the colony were equal. But the attitudes of mind and the feelings of superiority or resentment stemming from the days of the penal colony were not so easily set aside. Social distinctions, habits, and forms of speech (including pronunciation) remained. Even today, when the vast bulk of the white population is descended from free settlers who came long after the transportation of convicts ceased in the 1850s, social and cultural distinctions between a ruling class and a low-income wage-earning class remain. Most of the population exists somewhere between these two extremes, and many families include members from both the top and the bottom of the earning scale. But culturally there still exists a substantial division between those who patronise conventional high culture (opera, ballet, chamber and symphonic music, and serious poetry) and those who patronise popular culture (vaudeville and variety, pop concerts, and wrestling, for instance). Some cultural forms (television and rock music, for instance) are enjoyed by both groups, but even within this apparently common interest the selection of items and types of entertainment often reflects the wider cultural division.

The readership for serious, written poetry has always been small in Australia. A liking for poetry has, in fact, sometimes been seen as an indication of snobbery or effeminacy. At the same time there has been a much wider readership or audience for popular poetry in the form of sung or recited ballads (heroic, humorously anti-heroic, romantic, or subversive of authority). The two strands of poetry – literary and popular – began with the first settlers in 1788. What was written and composed in the early days of the colony was firmly based on English models, whether it consisted of loyal addresses in heroic couplets and thoughts on the strangeness and wildness of the new land or songs and ballads about defiant convicts and brutal authority.

As the nineteenth century went on, both strands of poetry often became aggressively nationalistic. Writers sought to distance themselves from English models in material and attitude, though not in the verse forms adopted. They tried to present an attitude to life that was Australian, which meant, in part, being anti-British and resentful of continuing British interference in the government of the several Australian colonies. It was often poetry about the harshness of life in the Australian bush, though it was largely written by city dwellers for city dwellers. (Even in the nineteenth century, Australia was one of the most urbanised of all countries.) One anonymous ballad, composed during the gold rushes of the second half of the century, suggests in a punning way that the 'mainstay' of Australia is 'stringy-bark and green-hide', two commodities almost indispensable in the country, but not much used in the cities. 'Stringy-bark' was one of the more prolific varieties of Australian eucalyptus or gum trees, which were cut down and used for making log huts as well as for firewood. 'Green-hide' was raw or untanned cattle hide, used in the bush for makeshift harness and wagon traces. The ballad composer emphasised the importance of both commodities in this way:

> Gold it is a precious thing, for commerce
>   it increases,
> But stringy-bark and green-hide, can beat it
>   all to pieces.
>
> *Chorus:*
> Stringy-bark and green-hide they will never
>   fail yer!
> Stringy-bark and green-hide are the mainstay
>   of Australia!

In the chorus, 'fail yer' is a representation of the way many Australians outside the ruling élite pronounce the words 'fail you'. In this way, a comic rhyme can be made with 'Australia' – otherwise a very difficult word to find a rhyme for.

Assertive nationalism eventually passed from Australian poetry. After the second world war – that is, in the generation to which Bruce Dawe belongs – Australian poetry lost its xenophobia. Literary poetry began to share in the experiments in versification that had occurred in other parts of the English-speaking world earlier in the twentieth century. In some ways the receptivity to international influences of a modernist kind appeared very quickly. Some Australian poets were at one and the same time assimilating the influences both of early twentieth-century leaders of modernism such as the Americans T.S. Eliot (1888–1965) and Ezra Pound (1885–1972) and of more recent American experimentalists such as Allen Ginsberg (*b*. 1926) and Frank O'Hara (1926-66). Their new experiences compressed, in other words, fifty years of development in the poetry of America and Britain.

Dawe's special place in Australian poetry

More than any other poet in Australia, Bruce Dawe has assimilated the influences of his generation of poets and combined them in a set of interests and a style that spread across from popular poetry into literary. He is the one contemporary poet who is genuinely literary and genuinely popular. He writes about matters of social, political and cultural interest to the great middle mass of the Australian population. He is almost the first poet to recognise that the typical Australian is not a bushman, a country landowner, a station hand (that is, an employee on a country estate or property), or an intellectual city dweller. The typical Australian is a person who lives neither in the country nor in the centre of a metropolis, but in one of the sprawling suburbs that grow and grow outward from the cities. Dawe writes about the interests such people have: the family car, television, football, their families, hire-purchase debts, B-grade American movies. He records such monuments of popular culture with an understanding and sympathy that avoid superiority and sarcasm. But he does not just record. Within the day-to-day life of his suburban characters he hints at and speculates on the philosophical nature and meaning of life. In 'Homo Suburbiensis', written in 1969, for instance, he writes about a suburban man standing in his vegetable garden among the tomatoes, the pumpkins, and the compost-box. He is standing by himself only vaguely aware of what his neighbours are doing, 'lost in a green confusion'. This is one of the few indications in the poem that Dawe is not locked into a popular frame of reference. As in many of his other poems, he spends most of the poem recording ordinary doings in ordinary language in a way that appeals to a wide range of readers. But he is a highly literate poet too. 'Lost in a green confusion' is an echo of the seventeenth-century English poet, Andrew Marvell (1621-78), that many of his readers might overlook. In his poem 'The Garden' Marvell wrote about the contemplative human mind withdrawing into itself. In its imagination it creates

> Far other worlds and other seas;
> Annihilating all that's made
> To a green thought in a green shade.

Marvell's thinker is in a largish secluded English garden, complete with fountain and sundial. Dawe's thinker is in a small suburban back garden, separated by a paling fence from his neighbours and well within earshot of their doings. But his thoughts are equally fundamental and wide-ranging, though less self-assured; he meditates on

> Not much but as much as any man can offer
> – time, pain, love, hate, age, war, death, laughter, fever.

This is the secret of Dawe's ability to interest both readers of literary poetry and a vast mass of people who do not normally care for poetry other than a few ballads and popular songs. He writes about the things most Australians are interested in, hints at the immense problems of life, and draws from his vast and omnivorous reading ideas and images that help to condense and vivify what he wants to say.

Dawe's life

Bruce Dawe has spent most of his life in two large country towns and one city in Australia. He was born on 15 February 1930 in Geelong, a large country town on the south coast of Victoria. He was the youngest of four children, his brother and two sisters being twenty or more years older than he. It was a poor family. Dawe has said that his father was

> a bit of a drifter. Dad wasn't around and when he was around he was just a nuisance. And the brother became like a father to me.*

But it was not an unliterary family. Dawe's mother was an uninhibited reciter of sentimental ballads such as 'The boy stood on the burning deck', 'The Child's First Grief' (both by Felicia Hemans (1793–1835)), 'Beth-Gêlart Or, The Grave of the Greyhound' and 'The Sale of the Pet Lamb'. Dawe's own redoubtable skill as a public reader of his poems may well have been influenced by her. His brother George, though he had had only six years of schooling, was an avid reader of westerns, thrillers and science fiction, tastes that Bruce Dawe acquired from him. And one of his sisters, Ethel, also with little schooling, wrote poetry that was published in metropolitan newspapers.

The family had several changes of house rather like the family in Dawe's poem 'Drifters'. During his primary schooling they moved to Melbourne. He went to secondary school at Northcote High School, where he completed his Intermediate Certificate, rather unhappily and discontentedly, in the commercial stream. His favourite subject was English. He read anything he could get his hands on. Between the ages of fourteen and fifteen he was reading great quantities of schoolboy thrillers, war stories, westerns (including the Hopalong Cassidy stories of Clarence Mulford (1883–1956) and work by Zane Grey (1872–1939)), science fiction (including H.G. Wells (1866–1946)), and detective and mystery stories (including Sir Arthur Conan Doyle (1859–1930)

---

* Interview with Roger McDonald, *Australian Writers on Tape*, University of Queensland Press, St Lucia, 1973.

and the two American authors who used the joint pseudonym Ellery Queen). In his school exercise books he used to write his own mystery stories. At the age of thirteen he began to write poetry, under the influence of writers as diverse as John Milton (1608–74), the English Romantics of the late eighteenth and early nineteenth centuries, Dylan Thomas (1914–53), and some contemporary Australian poets.

Halfway through 1946, at the age of sixteen-and-a-half, he left school to enter a solicitors' firm as a legal clerk. He had been unhappy both at school and at home. As he told Roger McDonald, he went through adolescence 'with a bit more than the ordinary amount of confusion and unhappiness along the line – I'm talking about the sort of domestic background in my own life'. No job lasted very long: he would be dismissed for lack of attention to his duties or would leave voluntarily. He worked as a salesman, a labourer in a saw-mill, office boy in an advertising agency and then advertising copywriter, office worker with Australian Estates, insurance salesman, and copyboy with two Melbourne newspapers, *Truth* and *The Sun*. Then he moved to the country to work as a labourer on a dairy farm. The work was hard, the companionship depressing, and the pay low. Returning to Melbourne he joined the Public Works Department as a labourer. This was the most stable job he had had: with some gaps in employment, he stayed with the Department until 1953. In terms of the people he met, and the colourful language he heard, it was a formative period, tuning his ear to the nuances and cadences of the speech of the ordinary Australian.

His reading and writing had continued uninterrupted. He read the thrillers of Raymond Chandler (1888–1959) and Dashiel Hammett (1894–1961); had some poems published in the 'Junior Age' (a section of the Melbourne daily newspaper, *The Age*) in 1947, using the pseudonym 'Llewellyn Rhys'; had poems published in the *Jindyworobak Anthology* in 1947, 1948 (in both years as 'Llewellyn Rhys'), and 1953; and continued writing stories.

At the age of eighteen he joined the Realist Writers, a group of generally left-wing social realist writers of whom Frank Kellaway (*b*. 1922) was the most influential. Dawe's active involvement was short-lived, though he continued to be impressed by Kellaway's colourful use of common speech in stories narrated in the first person.

He began going to night classes to gain the qualifications for adult matriculation into the University of Melbourne. At the 1953 examination he gained honours in English literature and a pass in French. In the following year he began his tertiary education at Melbourne Secondary Teachers' College and the University of Melbourne on a Victorian Education scholarship. At the university he met three other young poets, Chris Wallace-Crabbe (*b*. 1934), Vincent Buckley (*b*. 1925), and Philip Martin (*b*. 1931). Wallace-Crabbe's poem 'Losses and Recoveries' (in his *Where the Wind Came*, Angus & Robertson, Sydney, 1971) has a portrait of Dawe. In Wallace-Crabbe's recollection he is 'blue-chinned/ in military shirt and a maroon/figured art-silk tie', with a copy of John Ciardi's translation of Dante's *Inferno* (the great early fourteenth-century Italian poem) sticking out of the pocket of his jacket. Dawe, a few years older than most other students, was hailed as a literary find. He had had considerable experience of life and was writing from it, rather than from books. His language was colloquial and vernacular, his competence as a poet secure. Several of the friends he made were practising Catholics and it was in this year that he joined the Roman Catholic church. He became involved with university religious and political groups, enjoying student discussions and social life to the full. Between 1954 and 1962 the student publications, *Farrago, M.U.M.* and *Compass*, printed many of his poems and some of the early stories in a continuing series named after the young working-class narrator, Joey Cassidy. The full collection, eventually totalling twenty-one, was published by Penguin Books in 1983 under the title, *Over Here, Harv! and Other Stories*.

Wallace-Crabbe's poem recalls that 'In memory's yellow eye it's always summer,/nobody ever worked' and that there was endless discussion over coffee: 'coffee cups, unlike women, had no bottoms'. The distractions from strictly academic work were such that Dawe failed two of his four subjects and left the university. In 1955 he went to live with one of his sisters in New South Wales, working in a Sydney glass factory with European migrants as workmates, on the construction site of a new power-house, and in a factory making batteries.

In 1956 he returned to Melbourne and worked for three years in the Postmaster-General's Department (the PMG, now called Australia Post). He sorted mail and ended up as a postman delivering mail on an inner-city run. Roger McDonald recalls Dawe telling him that 'when he worked as a postman in suburban Melbourne he carried a mouth-organ with him on his run and played sentimental tunes to lonely old ladies'.*

Feeling the need to continue his formal education and to gain some discipline in his life, in 1959 he joined the Royal Australian Air Force (RAAF). After basic training (including weapons training) he began a radio course, but found it unsuitable and transferred to the education service. He spent most of his nine years in the RAAF working in libraries or (when overseas) helping to arrange schooling for airmen's families. He worked in Melbourne, Wagga (a New South Wales country town), and Toowoomba (a country town in Queensland, where he now lives).

* 'Sunday Night Radio: the Australian poet Bruce Dawe as seen by fellow poet Roger McDonald', broadcast by the Australian Broadcasting Commission on 19 September 1976.

It took Dawe another ten years to complete the Bachelor of Arts degree he had begun at Melbourne. Most of the work for his degree was done as a correspondence student at the University of Queensland. Dawe's choice of subjects, dictated by the limited selection available, is probably not significant: it included 'majors' in English literature and in history (British, Far Eastern, Australian, and USA) and some study of political science (government of Australia and the USA).

During this time his first book was published, he married, and his first child was born. *No Fixed Address* was published by Cheshire, Melbourne, in 1962. Its title poem had appeared in *M.U.M.* in 1954; it is the earliest poem retained in the collected volume, *Sometimes Gladness*. Dawe met his wife, Gloria Blain, while stationed in Toowoomba. They were married early in 1964. Their first child, Brian, born at the end of 1964, provided the subject for the title poem for another volume, *Condolences of the Season* (Cheshire, Melbourne, 1971).

Both *No Fixed Address* and Dawe's second volume, *A Need of Similar Name* (Cheshire, Melbourne, 1965), were published in editions of about 500 copies and quickly sold out. Both were well reviewed, and the second of them won for Dawe the first of many awards, the Myer Award for Australian Poetry.

In the first volume, the subject of death in several poems is balanced by a light-hearted whimsy in others. In the second volume there is a strong sense of political rage, directed against the brutality and crassness of big business and politicians. But that mood is also balanced by some tender love poems to his wife and the sense that rage needs to be tempered by patience. Both volumes contain many poems treating solemn historical and contemporary subjects in modern, vernacular, egalitarian language and other poems in which contemporary pomposity or heartlessness is exposed in mock-heroic language. In other words, Dawe is capable of using ordinary, even humorous, language to explain the genuinely solemn and of using mock-solemnity to expose the trivial. The second of these techniques is a form of satire; the first is sometimes so, when it is critical of false or over-reverent attitudes to serious matters.

EXERCISE:
Find and discuss examples of each of these techniques.

During 1964 and 1965 Dawe contributed a weekly verse column, 'Bard's Eye-View', to the Saturday edition of the daily paper, *The Toowoomba Chronicle*. Each week he found a news item that was absurd, funny, touching, or infuriating, and wrote a piece of light verse about the subject. Later examples of the same genre published in the same paper are collected in *Just a Dugong at Twilight* (Cheshire, Melbourne, 1975).

Dawe spent several months of 1966 in a posting to the RAAF base at Butterworth, on the mainland across from Penang, in Malaysia. In 'Butterworth Road' he records his sense of being a disliked tourist gazed at unblinkingly by the local people as the bus took servicemen to the ferry wharf for Penang. By this time Australian troops were committed to supporting the Americans in Vietnam, Australia being one of the very few countries to join America in this war. It was not a popular war in Australia and there were many protest rallies and marches. Dawe's anti-war poems date from this time.

By the end of 1966 he was back in Melbourne, beginning to enjoy considerable acclaim as a poet. In 1967 he won the $5000 Ampol Arts Award for Creative Literature. A journalist present at the award ceremony reported him as saying:

> This interest in the disreputable and the lesser subjects are [*sic*] central to me.... I'm not a great one for the blood red sunsets. There is so much of the incidental in life that is the subject for poetry and for humour.*

When he completed his RAAF service in mid-1968 Dawe used the remainder of the money from the Ampol Award to support himself and his family for the rest of the year. He completed his BA degree by correspondence and continued to write poetry.

His third volume, *An Eye for a Tooth*, was published by Cheshire in the same year. This time about 1000 copies were published. It is a volume that contains some of his most moving and funny poems. It is full of the helpless but genuinely sympathetic bystander's concern for what Dawe once called the 'bottom-dog', that is, the person who is by most social standards a complete failure.

Dawe was somewhat at a loose end after leaving the RAAF. His newly gained degree seemed not to improve his job prospects in Melbourne, where he worked as a mail-sorter and a Lands Tax Office clerk. In July 1969, however, he moved back to Toowoomba in a major change of career. He had been appointed as a teacher at Downlands College, a Catholic secondary school for boys. He had at last found a regular job that suited him. He taught at Downlands until the end of 1971, and in 1972 was appointed as a lecturer in literature at the Darling Downs Institute of Advanced Education, a tertiary institution in Toowoomba. In the same year his first postgraduate degree was awarded. It was a Bachelor of Letters degree, obtained by external study from the University of New England. The dissertation for the degree was 'Individual, Family and Society in the Plays of Arthur Miller'. Dawe later went on to obtain a Master of Arts degree and a Doctor

---

* *The Australian*, 11 March 1967, p. 26.

of Philosophy degree from the University of Queensland. The theses for these degrees were 'The Modern English Anti-Utopian Novel' (awarded 1975) and 'The Future on the Shelf: Obsession and Art in the Works of Graham Greene' (awarded 1980).

Dawe's fourth volume, *Beyond the Subdivisions*, was published by Cheshire at the end of 1969. In January 1970 he gave a paper at an arts and communications conference at the University of New England entitled 'The Sound-Proof Booth'. In it he said

> I generally prefer to develop one central image in a poem, spiralling inwards or outwards from the centre of it and trying by often a monologuic or casual-conversational effect to move the camera in or out without jogging to distraction the reader.*

He also commented on the insidious ubiquity of television and its tendency to blunt human sympathy through over-familiarity. Speaking of the use of old movies on television he said that 'Films and TV have been for years my staple fare' and 'I have seen more re-runs and re-runs of re-runs than I have read classics.'

In one of the poems of *Beyond the Subdivisions* ('A Week's Grace') he speaks of his own 'map-of-Australia profile' and of his emotions finding their way in life 'travelling, despairing, singing'.

EXERCISES:
1. Identify poems from *Beyond the Subdivisions* that match Dawe's description of how he organises a poem.
2. What evidence do you find in the poems of Dawe's addiction to films and television?

Seven of Dawe's poems were published in a pamphlet, *Heat-Wave*, by Sweeney Reed, Melbourne, 1970, but his next major publication was a retrospective selection of his best work. It was entitled *Condolences of the Season: Selected Poems* (Cheshire, Melbourne, 1971). 5000 copies were printed, but another 10,000 copies were needed in the following year. The book contains substantial selections from each of his earlier volumes, together with a number of new poems. With this publication there was no doubt of Dawe's position as a major contemporary Australian writer.

Dawe read nine of his poems in his compelling and inimitable way in *Bruce Dawe Reads From His Own Work* (Poets on Record 5, University of Queensland Press, St Lucia, 1971). The recording is accompanied by the text of the poems and some brief notes by the author.

The decade of the 1970s was not – at least until towards the end – a

---

* Quoted in Graeme Kinross Smith, 'Beyond the Subdivisions', *Idiom* [Victorian Association for the Teaching of English], July 1970, pp. 29–31.

particularly fruitful period for Dawe. Many of the poems are at the less weighty end of his range. Some of his light-verse contributions to *The Toowoomba Chronicle* were collected in *Just a Dugong at Twilight: Mainly Light Verse* (Cheshire, Melbourne, 1975). Five previously uncollected poems were included in Basil Shaw's helpful book, *Times and Seasons: An Introduction to Bruce Dawe* (Cheshire, Melbourne, 1974). One of the Joey Cassidy stories was also published for the first time in this volume.

In 1978 Dawe's poetry was issued in a collected edition entitled *Sometimes Gladness: Collected Poems, 1954–1978* (Longman Cheshire, Melbourne). This time the arrangement was thematic not chronological. Some critics objected to what they saw as a distracting and arbitrary ordering of the poems, but the purpose was clearly dictated by Dawe's experience as a teacher and lecturer. He himself had used a similar arrangement in an anthology of contemporary Australian poetry which he edited in 1974: *Dimensions* (McGraw-Hill, Sydney). In the Introduction to that book he justified the thematic organisation by saying:

> It has been necessary to depart from the traditional chronological ordering of poems, if poetry is to again seem what it is – a matter of concerns and obsessions which surround us like a sea whose depths surge and sway with the phases of the moon, our destiny. The sea within us responds to the sea outside us and it is this correspondence which is often the source of poetry. Lives are full of poetry and the many musics that inform it. (p. [x])

In the last few years, the targets of Dawe's satire have become narrower and more specific, and his satire is often much more bitter and less forgiving than it was earlier. When he was interviewed after the announcement that he was the recipient of the Patrick White Literary Award for 1980, he commented that he found it hard to identify issues as broad and highly emotive as the Vietnam War had been. 'But you can find them', he said. 'There's the computerised society, the silicon chip, the mind-freezing array of people-shaping techniques developed by scientists as irresponsible as scientists in the past who would develop something without knowing its full moral implications.'* Bruce Dawe's later satiric targets, however, have often been specific politicians and governments and the mood has been one of exasperation, bitterness, resentment, and even fury. It is sometimes as if Dawe were chafing at living in the city of Toowoomba and the state of Queensland. He says, however, that he is fascinated by the ratbag (eccentric, nonconformist, lacking common sense) and circus element in Queensland

---

* *Courier-Mail* (Brisbane), 22 November 1980, p. 18.

politics though 'The disadvantages of ringside seats are of course obvious, too: tigers with toothache, elephants with the "trots" ... '*

The second edition of *Sometimes Gladness*, subtitled *Collected Poems, 1954–1982*, was published by Longman Cheshire, Melbourne, in 1983. Thirty-one poems from the first edition were omitted, including the whole of the 'Topicalities' section drawn from *The Toowoomba Chronicle*. Forty-nine poems were added, all but four of them recent. The thematic arrangement of the first edition was not retained. Instead the poems were arranged in chronological order.

The later poems, in addition to revealing some sharp political satire, are also notable for their concentration on an awareness of ageing, renewed expressions of love, perhaps a more naked showing of sentiment, the plight of the Australian Aborigines, major ethical questions in Australia, the process of poetry writing, and renewed use of animals, birds, and insects as subjects. What might have seemed like a slackening of pressure in the early 1970s has vanished altogether.

Some of the new poems, together with several old favourites, were read with a commentary in the cassette, *Bruce Dawe Reads His Poems*, released by Longman Cheshire, Melbourne, in 1983. It is an invaluable aid to study.

Influences

Some of the main influences on Bruce Dawe's poetry may be summarised as follows:

(a) *Human experiences:*
 1. Early poverty
 2. Adolescent discontent
 3. A succession of semi-skilled and labouring jobs
 4. Excellent ear for common Australian speech
 5. Conversion to Roman Catholicism
 6. Service in RAAF
 7. Marriage and children
 8. Vietnam War
 9. Recognition and success as a writer
 10. Later work as teacher and lecturer
 11. Wide, almost undiscriminating, reading
 12. Films and television
 13. Queensland and Australian political events

---

* Bruce Bennett and Brian Dibble, 'An Interview with Bruce Dawe', *Westerly*, 24, No 4 (1979), 63–8 (p. 68).

(b) *Literary experiences:*
  1. Standard English classics: Milton, Keats, Hopkins
  2. Dylan Thomas
  3. Australian poetry of the 1940s as represented in the journal *Angry Penguins* and in the *Jindworobak Anthologies*
  4. Westerns, thrillers, science fiction (Zane Grey, Clarence Mulford, Oliver Strange, A.G. Hales, Ellery Queen, 'Sapper', W.W. Jacobs, (1863–1943), G.K. Chesterton (1874–1936), H.G. Wells)
  5. Modern short-story writers, including the Australian, Frank Kellaway, and the New Zealander, Frank Sargeson
  6. T.S. Eliot
  7. W.H. Auden
  8. Narrative and dramatic monologue poems in Geoffrey Moore (ed.), *The Penguin Book of Modern American Verse* (1954), especially those by Edgar Lee Masters (1869–1950), Edwin Arlington Robinson (1869–1935), and E.E. Cummings (1894–1962)
  9. Bertolt Brecht (1898–1956), Rainer Maria Rilke (1875–1926), Hugo von Hofmannsthal (1874–1929), Franz Werfel (1890–1945), Mascha Kaléko (1912–75), and other poets in *The Penguin Book of German Verse* (1957) and *Twentieth-Century German Verse* (Penguin, 1963)

A note on the text

The twenty poems discussed in detail are all to be found in Bruce Dawe, *Sometimes Gladness: Collected Poems, 1954–1982* (Longman Cheshire, Melbourne, 1983). Seventeen of them appear also in the first edition, *Sometimes Gladness: Collected Poems, 1954–1978* (Longman Cheshire, Melbourne, 1978). Thirteen are available in an earlier selection of Dawe's poetry, *Condolences of the Season: Selected Poems* (Cheshire, Melbourne, 1971). Page references to all three volumes are given in the summaries, in the order in which these volumes are given above.

Part 2
Summaries

A general summary of *Sometimes Gladness*

Sometimes Gladness: Collected Poems, 1954–1982 is Bruce Dawe's third retrospective collection of poems. The first, *Condolences of the Season* (1971), was arranged in chronological order, in accordance with the earlier individual volumes from which the poems were taken. The second, *Sometimes Gladness: Collected Poems, 1954–1978* (1978) was arranged according to thirteen themes, subjects, or types. Each of the thirteen sections was introduced by an imaginary epigraph or prefatory quotation providing a summary of the contents. In most books, such epigraphs would be genuine quotations, but Dawe exercised his impish humour and skill in parody to invent both the quotations and their supposed authors, as the (genuine) epigraph from Cervantes hints. (The dedication of the volume to the Blessed (now Saint) Maximilian Kolbe was, however, perfectly genuine and sincere. Father Kolbe was a Franciscan friar who during the German occupation of Poland volunteered to give his life in place of that of a condemned man who had a family. He was executed on 14 August 1941 in the Auschwitz concentration camp and canonised in 1982.) Epigraphs to individual poems were sometimes genuine (mostly when biblical or journalistic), sometimes fake (as with 'The Hill-Children' and 'The Gift of the Gods').

In what amounts to a substantially revised and augmented second edition of this earlier *Sometimes Gladness* volume, the 1983 volume reverts to a chronological order of poems. The dedication to St Maximilian Kolbe remains, but the fake epigraphs to sections have been deleted. An Index of Themes at the back of the volume largely follows the arrangement of the poems in the first edition, but it now contains eleven instead of thirteen sections: 'Dreams and Questions' now forms a single amalgamated section, and 'Topicalities' disappears with the omission of all the poems in this earlier section.

The eleven sections are:
City: a generally affectionate look at life in cities, with some poems specifically about Melbourne and Toowoomba
Suburbs: Dawe's sense of the mildly puzzling ordinariness of life and the vague feeling that it is somehow connected with the eternal are often apparent in these poems about life in the suburbs

Family affections: poems chiefly about the poet's own relatives
Friends and lovers: poems for and about himself, sometimes bearing on love affairs
Reflections: thoughts of a serious and comic nature about life and existence. Some are sententious, others (for example, 'Life ... can be a bit of a bastard') so expressed in Dawe's characteristic mode of speech that they are both amusing and provocative. Films, television, zoos, and wrestling are all employed as material
War: mostly seen from a distance or before or after battle. Despite vivid local detail, there is a strong sense of war as a depressing continuous state in human history
Private fates: a wide assortment of individuals comes face-to-face with questions about morality, meaning, or the pursuit of happiness. Concern and pathos, combined with a sense of helplessness, are often present
Images: sharply visualised experiences, mostly with a background of Australian scenery, used as starting points for reflections about the meaning of life
Elegies: reminiscences of the deaths of various people, combining pathos, humour, and celebration. There is an elegiac element in many other poems which are not included in this section
Callings: the writing of poetry and other occupations used as images for existence and meaning
Dreams and Questions: the dreams are more like nightmares – in the sense that they are true reports but Dawe would prefer that they were not. This is true of many of the political poems. A few poems are in a lighter mood, with touches of surrealistic exaggeration. The questions are a mixed collection of poems, mostly satiric

At the back of the volume there is an Index to Forms which divides the poems into the broad formal categories of blank verse, quatrains, other rhymed forms, sonnets, dramatic monologues, and free verse. Each poem is listed under only one category, though it should be realised that the dramatic monologues are mostly written in blank verse or free verse.

Detailed summaries of selected poems

'Enter Without So Much As Knocking', pp. 11–12 (*Sometimes Gladness*, 1978, pp. 6–7; *Condolences*, pp. 6–7; *Bruce Dawe Reads*, pp. 1–3)

A 1959 poem in free verse, influenced in subject and style by 'Dirge', by the American poet Kenneth Fearing (1902–61). Dawe presents a detached mechanistic view of human life. The reader is intended to protest 'But there must be more to it than that!' The poem is framed by what Dawe has called 'parentheses to a life'. He was thinking of the blinking or flickering of neon signs (which are sometimes found outside hospitals), symbolising the uncertainty and transience of life. Another way of considering the 'Blink, blink' is as the movement of eyelids blinking as they gaze on the world and on death. The biblical expression, 'in the twinkling of an eye', referring to the Last Judgment, may also be recalled. In addition, the 'Blink, blink' could be the movement of a car's traffic indicators signalling a turn, a turn that is literally into a street where a sign says 'HOSPITAL. SILENCE' or 'CEMETERY' and metaphorically into life or death.

Life between birth (in the maternity hospital) and death (in the cemetery) is marked by the trivial evidence of the popular culture and authoritarian signs that make up so much of most people's lives. Dawe draws examples from television, advertising, films, and the attitudes people adopt when they get into their cars. The common man or Everyman who is the subject of the poem dies as a passenger in a car driven by his wife Alice and is buried in a cemetery described in terms of the absence of the minor problems and frustrations of life (parking tickets, television personalities, hire purchase, bad breath, and so on). That is all life and death seem to mean.

NOTES AND GLOSSARY:
title: the imagery of William Blake (1757–1827) and William Wordsworth (1770–1850) about the soul entering life and the biblical imagery of entering the kingdom of heaven are made to seem almost literally true. But in Dawe's poem life and death seem so insignificant as rooms to enter that no knock is needed or would be noticed. The title is almost the wording that might be seen on an office door
epigraph: (*Latin*) from Genesis 3:19, 'Remember, O man, that thou art dust, and unto dust shalt thou return...'
Bobby Dazzler: an imaginary television compère on Channel 7 (an actual channel) with a line of mindless patter. In obsolete slang a 'bobby dazzler' is a thing or person exceptionally good or striking (for example, a tremendous kick in football or an enormous black eye)
Anthony Squires: an actual brand of men's suits in Australia
Coolstream-Summerweight: the sort of name given to a lightweight suit by manufacturers to make it seem attractive

Summaries · 21

Junior Department: another term borrowed from a large department store (where it refers to children's or adolescents' clothing) and applied by Dawe to the family
Luck's... Quiz: an imaginary give-away programme of the type popular on Australian television in the 1960s
Reno's: a used-car saleyard
(beep): the sound of a car horn operated by a driver irritated with traffic congestion. As '(beep beep)' it here represents also the sound used on radio and television to black out an expletive as in 'What the...'
drive-in: open-air cinema where viewers watch a large screen from their own parked cars
hit... down: common strategy in a street brawl; here used as a metaphor for an approach to life
Jim: presumably Jim Jessup, Clare's husband, whose house the central character and his wife are visiting
soiled: dramatic irony, in view of the burial he is shortly to undergo
Probity: not an actual undertaker's name, but representative of the trustworthy image they try to achieve
automatic... winding: the beginning of a revival of the car imagery, which continues to the end
residentials: a term generally used in Australia for cheap boarding-houses
down-payments: deposits for purchasing goods on credit
halitosis: bad breath

QUESTIONS:
1. What materials are used both in the first and in the last verse-paragraph? What effect does this have?
2. Why is the last 'Silence' not in capitals?

'Letting Go of Things', p. 14 (*Sometimes Gladness*, 1978, p. 64; *Condolences*, p. 5)

A meditative poem of 1960 in free verse (with some blank verse lines) that is given shape not just by regular rhythm and the flow of ideas but also by idea-patterns such as 'death... end... abrupt' and by sound-patterns such as 'involuntary... poetry'. Dawe discusses the moments at the end of the day when one lets go the concerns of the day, allows one's consciousness to drift away, and becomes subject to the unconscious and involuntary part of the mind, the Id. It is like a factory having ceased work for the day and been handed over to the nightwatchman.

Sleep is seen, in a commonplace of meditative thought, as a preparation or rehearsal for death. Dawe's Christian belief is expressed in the notion of prostrating the soul before God, regarding death as a 'sacrament', and in the pious hope that he is in God's care during sleep. His interest in the poetic imagination is expressed in the romantic images of the second verse-paragraph: sleep brings dreams of youth, love, energy, and magnificent success.

NOTES AND GLOSSARY:
prostration: in Catholic worship, a complete abasement of the body, indicating greater humility than ordinary kneeling for prayer
sacrament: in Christian theology a means by which God's grace is made available through a ceremony. Anointing before death (Extreme Unction) is one of the seven sacraments, but the word can be applied to any outward action that has an inner meaning. Death is the outward sign of the release of the spirit or soul and its return to the eternal world
Id: Latin 'it', used originally in translating German psychoanalytic theory about primitive, instinctive energies of the unconscious mind
confederate: here ally or colleague. The United States Civil War (1861–5) was fought between the Union and the Confederate States. The motto of the Union, 'In God we trust', may have suggested this line
quicksilver: literally mercury, but here a word used for its romantic associations of mystery and fleetingness
impossible: sublime, normally unattainable when awake

QUESTIONS:
1. What parallels do you see in idea and structure between the two verse-paragraphs?
2. How important are the polysyllabic words, for example, prostration, acquiescence, luminosities, involuntary? How do they fit in with more everyday expressions such as 'letting go', 'garrulous old night-watchman', 'something for an old man to doze over'?

'The Flashing of Badges', p. 18 (*Sometimes Gladness*, 1978, p. 210; *Condolences*, p. 27)

A 1962 poem in blank verse (unrhymed lines of about ten syllables, four or five of them being stressed). It concerns the attitudes of dead-beats and attitudes toward them. A dead-beat in the USA and in Australia is an out-of-work man without a home who is likely to pick food-scraps out of garbage bins and cigarette butts out of the gutter. He will avoid outright begging but will engage passers-by in conversation hoping that the pathetic story of his life will result in a gift of money. The money is likely to be spent on liquor.

Dawe is sympathetic and understanding, prepared, even eager, to offer money, but, like most people, anxious to disengage himself from the obligation to listen further. He begins by observing the typical dead-beat's type of salesmanship: he will present himself as having the same background and ideas as the person accosted, whether obviously a serviceman, a Catholic, or a student (Dawe was, of course, all three). To allege a connection with scholarship might be the most difficult of the three, so Dawe engages in a complex simile and metaphor comparing the dead-beat's revelation of literacy 'somewhere in his family' to a child's opening his hand to display a pet frog to an adult who pretends to be amazed. What is in the family is merely 'literacy', the ability to read, which the dead-beat, from his limited education, seems to think is the equivalent of being a university student.

The listener would be only too glad to give the dead-beat money with some comment about the unjustness of life. But this will not satisfy the dead-beat and will, says Dawe, do him double harm. One harm appears to be unstated: that the offering of money will send the dead-beat, dejected rather than elated, to the nearest pub to spend it on liquor. More importantly, however, the harm done will be to withdraw the dead-beat's frail hold on self-respect and dignity. He dwells on the fringe of respectable society and his story is an attempt to make another person believe in him. It is a slight hope, for the facts of his appearance are in flat contradiction of the idealised story he tells. But he needs to cling to the possibility of presenting himself as a worthwhile human being, and dismissal by a gift of money is not what he wants or needs.

NOTES AND GLOSSARY:

title: men commonly wear badges in the lapels of their jackets to indicate their beliefs and affiliations. This was a practice very common in Australia in the 1950s and 1960s, where one saw many badges to indicate war veterans, Rotarians, and various kinds of Christian organisations. These could be displayed ('flashed') with pride or superiority or in an attempt to attract the notice of a fellow believer

uniform: servicemen's uniform

old digger: war veteran, digger being the common word for a soldier in Australia (perhaps from the amount of time he spends digging trenches)

24 · Summaries

Mass: the main Catholic service of worship

loyal as hell: very devout; but the dead-beat's choice of simile is inept and unlikely to impress the person addressed because he is comparing religious faith to hell

corduroys: trousers of ribbed cotton material, much worn by university students

grimace: screwing up the face; suggestive of the dead-beat's weather-worn features and also perhaps of his slight puzzlement at how to ingratiate himself with a student

learning's obscure god: Dawe's comment about the difficulty of knowing what the objective of learning is or what the principles are that govern knowledge

squatting: like a frog. The word is also used in Australia for the position adopted in order to defecate in the bush and for the act of occupying land without a legal right: both senses suggest something odd or irregular about the dead-beat's claim to be associated with learning

magnanimous: generous

bleary: blurred, as from sleeplessness, tiredness, or drunkenness

Tierra del Fuego: the bleak southern tip of South America (the Spanish name meaning land of fire); the edge of civilisation, metaphorically applied to the limits of dignity and self-respect

herb of deception: a herb is a pleasant-smelling plant that might just grow in a sheltered corner of a bleak land. The chances are slight, just as the chances of the dead-beat being able to convince the listener of his worth are slight. To do so would be a kind of deception, because his self-respect and esteem have almost gone. The truth of the matter is as bleak as the very winds of Tierra del Fuego, and shows him to have almost no admirable qualities

topsoil: the surface layer of soil that contains almost all the nutrients essential to support plant life. Dawe sees the value that we place on a human being as like the topsoil on the earth. It can, however, be washed away, and every time a dead-beat is treated with indifference a little more of the topsoil or value washes away (that is, 'sluices')

Summaries · 25

QUESTIONS:
1. Why is the flashing of his badge the first thing that the dead-beat does?
2. Whom is the dead-beat trying to deceive?

'And a Good Friday Was Had By All', p. 38 (*Sometimes Gladness*, 1978, p. 192; *Condolences*, p. 41)

A dramatic monologue in free verse written in 1964. It is spoken by a Roman non-commissioned officer, perhaps a centurion, in charge of the crucifixion of Jesus, the Christian God. Unlike most of Dawe's dramatic monologues this one gives no clear indication of who is being addressed. It seems to be a story told later to a thoughtful, sympathetic audience, but at the beginning and end the Roman soldier seems to be telling the story to himself. (According to St Mark's Gospel 15:39, the centurion at the crucifixion said 'Truly this man was the Son of God'.) He is a man whose tender feelings have not been coarsened by his job. He is in fact rather resentful of the Roman imperial system that employs him.

With his assistant, Silenus, he goes about the task of crucifying Jesus. As in the New Testament Gospel accounts, there are women present and he orders them to be kept back. He hammers in the spikes that peg the body to the cross, apologises to Jesus for having to do it, then hauls on ropes to bring the cross upright. He notices the various reactions of the bystanders, some satisfied by the outcome of their plotting, some inquisitive, the women genuinely concerned, and a blind man (who had hoped for a miracle to cure him if Jesus had lived) weeping.

NOTES AND GLOSSARY:
title: Good Friday is the name given by Christians to the day Jesus was crucified. The title is a parody of the common saying about a party or other celebration where people have enjoyed themselves, perhaps excessively: 'a good time was had by all'

God Almighty...: not so much a statement that the person who lay down on the cross was God as an expletive invoking the name of God in astonishment that the condemned man willingly lay down without being forced. The account accords with the biblical interpretation of Jesus as a voluntary sacrifice

Silenus: in Greek mythology the name of a satyr (grotesque combination of man and beast who appeared in fertility rites) who was the companion of Dionysus (Bacchus); he was elderly, drunken, and debauched, but also wise, jovial, and fond of music. Keats refers to him in *Endymion*, IV, 215–17. But Dawe probably just uses it as a common Roman name

nice work: sarcastic; the work is the very opposite of 'nice'. Silenus is also making the point that the work is inappropriate for soldiers, but the trouble is that once you sign 'on the dotted line', that is join the army, you have to do what you are told without complaint

Ave Caesar: Hail Caesar, the common salute to the Roman emperor

malarkey: nonsense, rubbish

Imperator Rex: Emperor King, two titles of the Roman emperor. Pontius Pilate, who condemned Jesus to death by crucifixion, also commanded that the cross should bear a sign announcing that he was 'Iesus Nazarenus Rex Iudaeorum' – Jesus of Nazareth the King of the Jews

Nazarene: of Nazareth, the town where Jesus was brought up

kick up a fuss: complain, struggle

do your block: Australian slang for lose your temper

bones give way: St John's Gospel denies this: 'A bone of him shall not be broken' (19: 36), but this is improbable and even if it were so the centurion might not have noticed

Orders is orders: a common (if ungrammatical) saying when carrying out an embarrassing or unpleasant task

wasn't a patch on: was nothing in comparison with. 'Wasn't' completes the line so that attention is drawn to the assertion that the drill-sergeant was not God

springboard: flexible board from which a diver projects himself into the water. A diver often (in a swallow dive) spreads his arms out. The emphasis here is on gracefulness and unflinching command of the elements of air and water

whole damned creation: 'damned' is an imprecation, but also literally true according to Christian theology, for the whole world would be damned except for the sacrificial death of Jesus

had it in for: had a grudge against

QUESTIONS:
1. What evidence is there that the centurion's tone is one of resignation and weariness?
2. Are there any touches of humour in this poem?

Summaries · 27

'Condolences of the Season', p. 39 (*Sometimes Gladness*, 1978, p. 39; *Condolences*, p. 52)

A 1964 monologue addressed by the poet to his new-born son. It is in blank verse. True blank verse is unrhymed, but in this poem there are occasional rhymes and half-rhymes (for example, son, come, mums; countenance, instance; yes, Ted's; foul, frail). Dawe imagines a pleasant conspiracy between himself and his male child against the sentimental fussing of the women ('a matronly cosmogony of mums') who 'hover above your pram or basinette'. The women gush over the baby and try to trace in his features resemblances to those of older members of the family. Even when he reaches middle age the boy will still not be safe from an even older member of the family detecting a family likeness. The beginning and end of the poem have images of formal religion: alleluia, ritual... heretical. The third stanza reinforces the sense of conspiratorial comradeship between father and son against the rest of the world in imagery of escape and detection.

NOTES AND GLOSSARY:

title: congratulations are normally offered on the birth of a child, but Dawe thinks 'condolences' (that is sympathy, as after death) are more appropriate

diddums: baby-talk used by adults, often as a substitute for 'Did you' as in 'Diddums want to burp, eh?'

ickle-man: baby-talk for 'little man'. Children have particular difficulty in enunciating the 'l' sound, and often omit it when they are learning to talk

alleluia: from a Hebrew exclamation of praise to the deity, 'Praise ye the Lord'. Here used to suggest an ecstatic cry of adoration addressed to the baby

grand-dam: grandmother

crabbed: here meaning wrinkled like a crab-apple

infant-elderly: young children are often said to resemble old men because they are wrinkled and rather shapeless

cosmogony: strictly, the formulation of a theory about the origin of the universe, but here used humorously as a collective noun of assembly to suggest a vast number of women, perhaps rather massive in shape

mums: a common name for 'mothers'

pram: the common word in Australia for perambulator or baby-carriage

basinette: bassinet, a cradle

Identi-Kitted: Police use the Identi-Kit system of individual facial

28 · Summaries

features drawn on transparent sheets to build up portraits of wanted criminals from verbal descriptions. The women gushing over the baby are said to use an analogous system of matching parts of relatives' faces to produce a portrait of the baby. Dawe facetiously suggests that the system never allows the criminal (the baby) to escape, no matter how he tries to disguise himself as he grows older

thatching: longer hair for men, covering the ears, was just coming into fashion in Australia when Dawe wrote this poem. He suggests it looks like a thatched roof (that is, one made of straw or reeds) extending over the ears

lard: pig's fat, as used in cooking. The word is sometimes used to describe human fat, as in the unflattering description of a fat person as 'a tub of lard'

pack: a pack of bloodhounds on the scent. The notion of their sniffing for a scent makes the old relatives's outcry 'Harry's nose!' particularly apt

octogenarian: a person aged eighty or more

bunny-rug: a baby's blanket, often embroidered or appliquéd with rabbits (bunnies)

burping: belching, especially when induced in a baby after a feed

heretical: unorthodox in faith, because the baby is in league with his father against the semi-religious baby-worship of the women

QUESTIONS:
1. Is the author contemptuous or resigned about the women's behaviour?
2. What is the effect of the several instances of rhyme and half-rhyme, especially in the last two lines?

'The Not-So-Good Earth', p. 66 (*Sometimes Gladness*, 1978, p. 194; *Condolences*, p. 55; *Bruce Dawe Reads*, p. 7)

A dramatic monologue of 1966 in free verse, again with little sense of the audience being addressed by the speaker. He is one of a family watching on television a re-run of the 1937 MGM movie, *The Good Earth*. This is based on Pearl Buck's (1892–1973) Pulitzer Prize-winning novel of 1931, which deals with the struggle of the poor Chinese peasant and his wife during the first two decades of this century to become rich land-owners through hard work on the soil they worship. They survive hardship, famine, flood, drought, disease, banditry and civil war. One major scene concerns the flight of the Manchus in the face of the declaration of a republic (in 1912). The Manchu artillery rides at breakneck speed through the city market, gun carriages recklessly knocking down the terrified bystanders. A little earlier in the film (Dawe has transposed the order) the peasant family is reduced to eating roots dipped in earth warmed in a cooking pot. The film does not actually have a scene with the death of a grandmother, but Dawe is concerned to make two main points: the trivialising of even the most solemn matters by their association with forceful advertising and the Australian viewer's lack of patience with Confucian stoicism.

The family watching the screen is representative of the West trying, but not too hard and with little intelligence, to understand the East. The father's accidental and farcical action in cutting off the film is of no great consequence to the viewers: they are interested only in the superficial action, not the meaning.

NOTES AND GLOSSARY:
25-inch: a popular size of television screen in Australia
comfort: the comfort is that of the viewers, but the effect of television is to transfer one's own physical comfort to one's attitude even to the most wretched scenes of human misery, so that they fail to make any impact except as entertainment
convex glass: the curved television screen
contrast knob: the means of adjusting the television picture to emphasise (or blur) the distinction between the dark and the light parts of the image. Uncle Billy likes to have sharp contrast, so that he can see the shapes better
Confucian analects: the *Analects* is a collection of teachings attributed to Confucius (*c*. 551–?479BC), the Chinese sage whose work is chiefly about correct conduct which leads to good government; the sayings can seem platitudinous to non-Chinese readers
suspenseful: full of excitement and speculation about what is to happen next
break: an interruption of the film in order to show advertisements; common on US and Australian television
plug: here advertisement or 'commercial', which includes in this instance a symphony orchestra playing, rather incongruously, to recommend a brand of cigarette

Craven A: a popular brand of cigarette
neat as a whistle: without fuss or mess
main lead: the electrical connection to the power socket
inscrutable: a word commonly applied by the Western world to Chinese, who seem mysterious, unfathomable. Its literal meaning is 'incapable of being examined': this is also true of the television screen, which now cannot be watched, and of television generally, even when working, because it presents a bland, uncomprehending picture of reality
Dad: common name for 'father'
curlicue: fanciful twist

QUESTIONS:
1. What Western prejudices about the Chinese does the poem reveal?
2. Do you consider the ending farcical? Does it damage the serious message of the poem?

'A Victorian Hangman Tells His Love', p. 74 (*Sometimes Gladness*, 1978, p. 171; *Condolences*, p. 70; *Bruce Dawe Reads*, pp. 11-12)

A dramatic monologue of 1967, chilling because of the intimate tone adopted towards a macabre subject, an execution by hanging. The hangman speaks to his victim like an infatuated, solicitous bridegroom to his bride. Ronald Ryan was the last person judicially hanged in Australia. The Premier of Victoria's announced intention to proceed with the sentence in 1967 created a great controversy between supporters and opponents of the death sentence. Dawe's poem is clearly on the side of abolition.

The speaker, the hangman in his grotesque uniform, lovingly and soothingly leads the condemned prisoner from his cell to the scaffold. He binds the arms, makes the formal offer to deliver a last statement, places the rope noose over the neck and adjusts the canvas hood on the head of the victim. He speaks in the language of marriage ('nuptials', 'consummation', 'heart', 'wed', 'ring', 'altar') as he goes about his gruesome work. The end will be, from the speaker's point of view, not 'death' – a word not mentioned in the poem – but 'darkness' and 'new life' and a newspaper report.

In a lecture entitled 'The Sound-Proof Booth' given at the University of New England in 1970, Dawe spoke at some length of this poem. His vision of the public events that inspired it was as follows:

> The drama I saw being played out was one where an unholy macabre union of two souls took place on the scaffold – the peculiar intimacy

of the relationship of executioner and victim, both masked, like lovers at some inhuman masquerade ball, the one, unlike most of us knowing the day, hour, minute of his death as well as the means ('punishment', 'example', etc.) the other doing a job... bound to each other in a public consummation as significant in its way as that attending any royal nuptials.*

'The Sting' and 'On the Death of Ronald Ryan' are on the same subject.

NOTES AND GLOSSARY:

title:	reminiscent of W.B. Yeats's (1865–1939) title for a poem, 'An Irish Airman Foresees his Death' and of Shakespeare's phrases in *Twelfth Night*, II.4: 'Tell her my love' (Duke Orsino, line 80), 'She never told her love' (Viola, line 109). 'Victorian' refers to the Australian state of Victoria, the government of which ordered the hanging to take place. 'Tells' is used in the sense of 'announces' or 'confesses'
State's:	the State is the government of Victoria
nuptials:	an elevated term for the marriage ceremony
consummation:	the bizarre notion that the hangman's entry into the condemned cell is like physical entry after marriage
ask...say:	the conventional opportunity for a last speech by the condemned. In the marriage ceremony there is a similar opportunity for the man and woman to declare any reason why the marriage should not take place
tranquilliser:	Ryan did in fact reject the offer of a sedative or soporific. In 'The Sting' Dawe writes about an injection given by the prison doctor
breath:	the essence of life, as speech is the essence of *human* life, but both are presented by the hangman as impediments which 'distract' us from our true end, that is, death
heirloom:	treasured object handed down in a family from one generation to the next
holy family:	the previous three people hanged in Victoria were a woman and two men convicted of killing a bookmaker by torture. The Christian holy family

---

* In I.V. Hansen, ed., *Bruce Dawe: The Man Down the Street*, Victorian Association for the Teaching of English, Melbourne, 1972, p. 46.

lovers' tree: consists of Mary, Jesus, and Joseph – a woman and two men. The hangman's grotesque imagination sees no incongruity in the analogy
a tree on which lovers carve their names or initials. The softwood beam from which the rope hangs has been cut into by the 'heirloom' rope on the three previous occasions it has been used

officially prescribed darkness: the sentence of death prescribed by the court

clean bill of health: many 'modern brides' go for a medical check-up before marriage to see whether there will be any complications in pregnancy and childbirth

With this spring: a parody of the bridegroom's words in the marriage service: 'With this ring I thee wed...'. The hangman, having positioned the condemned man on the trapdoor, leaps to the lever that opens the trapdoor and thus allows the body to dangle on the rope

QUESTIONS:
1. How effective is Dawe's poem in producing a horror of execution in the reader?
2. Does the hangman become more intimate and excited as the poem progresses? What is the evidence?

'Life-Cycle', p. 81 (*Sometimes Gladness*, 1978, p. 180; *Condolences*, pp. 66-7)

A humorous free-verse poem of 1967 arranged in tercets (groups of three lines) that represent syntactical units. Dawe grew up in the state of Victoria, where a local type of football (Australian Rules) absorbs almost the entire population during the winter months. A quasi-religious fervour grips almost all Victorians, who attach their loyalty to one or other of the clubs playing in the Victorian Football League competition in Melbourne, the capital city. Each club has distinctive colours, which are displayed on ribbons, banners, scarves, hats, motorcars, balloons, and so on. Unlike other football games which are played in two equal halves of the allotted time, Australian Rules is played in four quarters (perhaps to minimise any advantage resulting from Melbourne's rapidly changing weather).

Membership of clubs, which gives entry to the best seating and other privileges, is eagerly sought. Children are often placed on a waiting list at birth. In this poem Dawe follows a club supporter's life through from birth to old age. In his cradle (cot) he is wrapped in the colours of

Summaries · 33

the club his father supports. His first cries are interpreted as 'carn' (that is 'Come on', the common cry of support for a team, as it sounds when shouted at a match). When still small he is taken to view a match on his father's shoulders. This is a kind of initiation for children, marking the end of childish innocence, as they listen to crude language and eat typical football snacks. Even their engagements and marriages are likely to be dictated by the success of their team.

The sense of being born into a religion and automatically following its rituals is reinforced by references to 'pure flood of sound', 'scarfed with light', 'voice of God', 'covenant', and so on. Word order and diction reminiscent of the Bible are used in 'Hot pies and potato-crisps they will eat', 'forswear', 'cling to', and 'behold'. From then on to the end of the poem, the ideas and language are largely religious and ceremonial. 'Tides of the home-team's fortunes', the suspension of time, the continuity of faith, the mythology of fertility rituals whereby life is renewed each year (at the beginning of the football season rather than in spring), the unchanging dance, and the 'hope of salvation' are all examples of this religious fervour among football devotees. 'Salvation', the last word of the poem, thus completes the biography of the devotee, which began in the cradle.

The poem uses religious imagery to satirise the mania for football, but it is indulgent, understanding, whimsical satire, not at all bitter or condemnatory.

NOTES AND GLOSSARY:

title: a reference to both the span of an individual's life from cradle to grave and the recycling of human life from generation to generation

dedication: Big Jim Phelan, a committee-member of the Collingwood Football Club, a notably large and volatile supporter of their games, usually dressed in a pyjama suit of black and white six-inch squares (Collingwood's colours – they are known as the Magpies). Dawe knew him through friendship with his younger son, Barry, whom he met at Melbourne University. The poem 'Big Jim' is a tribute to this man, 'whom I loved like a father' says Dawe in *Bruce Dawe Reads His Poems*

beribboned: adorned with ribbons in club colours. There is an echo here of 'Vitaï Lampada' by Sir Henry Newbolt (1862–1938), a poem about schoolboy sport and patriotism, with its motive for doing well – 'And it's not for the sake of a ribboned coat'

barracking: loud vocal support and encouragement for a team

rusk: crisp biscuit, given to babies when they are getting their first teeth; parents play a game pretending to take the rusk from a baby's mouth

Tiger: supporter of the Richmond Football Club in Melbourne, which has black and gold colours like a tiger's stripes; also a name often given with fondness or exasperation to a rough or difficult young boy

League: The Victorian Football League controls the major competition

empyrean: the highest heaven, here applied to a football match, which is 'roaring' with the shouts of the crowd

shrapnelled: fragmented, broken open

streamers...scarfed: streamers and scarves in club colours are very prominent at a football match

bludger: Australian slang for someone who works very little or who relies on someone else's work

covenant: solemn agreement, particularly between God and his Chosen People; the boy has become one of the faithful now

Hot pies and potato-crisps: these are customary snacks at football games

forswear: renounce, reject, as in the solemn renunciation of a false religion or of sin by the faithful. In Christian baptism a promise is made to 'renounce the devil and all his works'

Demons: another name for devils, appropriate to 'forswear'; the popular nick-name of Melbourne Football Club

Saints: popular nick-name of St Kilda Football Club

ladder: football table or competition scale; a team goes up the ladder each time it wins a game. 'Heaven' is here imagined as winning the Grand Final

home-team: the one you support and barrack for

one-point win: scoring in Australian Rules is very high (often over a hundred points to each team). A win by one point would be unusually exciting

They...old: an echo of the poem 'For the Fallen' by Laurence Binyon (1869–1943), often recited at gatherings of war veterans: 'They shall grow not old, as we that are left grow old'

more northern States: New South Wales and Queensland where Australian Rules is not played much

three-quarter-time: the interval before the last quarter of the match is played, a particularly exciting stage, especially if the scores are level
term: another name for quarter
race-memory: a subconscious attitude passed on from generation to generation
welter: turmoil, muddle
boundary-fence: the fences separating the playing field from the spectators
lions: Lions is the name for Fitzroy, a team once supported by Dawe and hence said to be reinvigorated (resurgent) through the poem
centaur-figures: the centaur is a mythological creature, half man and half horse – appropriate in speed and perhaps sexual drive as a metaphor for footballers; but the main point is the folk-memory and the folk-mythology that keep the game alive
Chicken Smallhorn: Wilfred 'Chicken' Smallhorn, a small man who was well-known as a radio and television commentator on the game. Formerly a player for Fitzroy club and on one occasion a winner of the Brownlow Medal for 'best and fairest' player of the season
maize-god: the chief figure in ancient fertility rites concerned with the annual growth of crops. Often a youth was chosen each year to take part (and sometimes be sacrificed) in the rite – hence the figure symbolising eternal youth had 'a thousand shapes'. Dawe fancifully imagines that Chicken Smallhorn, coming into prominence each year at the start of the season, presiding over the rites of the season like a priest, and disappearing into obscurity at the end of it, has a life like that of the maize-god figure
six-foot recruit: a new player six feet tall (not particularly tall, in fact, for this type of football)
Eaglehawk: a Victorian country town. Melbourne football survives as a major spectacle by recruiting promising players from country teams

QUESTIONS:
1. What evidence is there that the game is considered more important than the individuals concerned with it?
2. Do you find the imagery of religious ritual effective?

'Homecoming', p. 92 (*Sometimes Gladness*, 1978, p. 90; *Condolences*, p. 77; *Bruce Dawe Reads*, p. 10)

A free-verse poem of 1968, with a high proportion of a repeated rhythmical pattern x/xx/ (unaccented, accented, unaccented, unaccented, accented: as in 'they're bringing them in'). In February 1968 the United States and South Vietnamese troops in Vietnam began to suffer heavy casualties at the hands of the National Liberation Front army (the Viet Cong) and the North Vietnamese who launched a series of major attacks known as the Tet offensive (Tet being the Vietamese name for the lunar new year, normally a holiday period). Australian troops were fighting alongside the Americans and they also suffered heavy losses. Dawe has said* that he was gripped by two items in the American weekly news magazine *Newsweek*. One was a front colour cover showing a US tank returning to base with dead and dying soldiers draped over it. The other was a report of arrangements at Oakland Airforce Base in California for transport planes to take off with fresh loads of troops for Vietnam and to return with the dead bodies.

This poem deals with the various stages in the return of the dead, specifically from Vietnam, but in general from any modern war. It is a lament for the futility of war expressed in the detail of the Vietnam War. Dawe writes of tanks, trucks, green plastic bags, the mortuary, deep-freeze lockers, and giant transport planes taking off from Vietnam and then arriving in the homelands of the soldiers to a wail of lamentation. The words 'They're bringing them home' and its several variations act as a moving cry of lament through the poem.

NOTES AND GLOSSARY:
Grants: a type of US tank
zipping ... bags: a form of temporary storage and transportation for dead soldiers, known as 'body bags'
Saigon: capital of South Vietnam, penetrated by Viet Cong guerillas during the Tet offensive
deep-freeze lockers: the next stage of the journey of the dead
Tan Son Nhut: American air base near Saigon
noble: a word often applied to dogs or hounds. Dawe's imagination has perhaps been stimulated by the word 'deep-freeze' into thinking of noble dogs who rescue wounded skiers in countries of ice and snow. The transport planes, here compared to dogs, are later, at the end of their journey, compared to skiers

* *English Teachers Association (NSW) Newsletter*, Sydney, Australia, February 1980, pp. 4–5.

kinky-hairs:	black Americans, with tightly curled hair
crew-cuts:	close-cropped hair styles
non-coms:	non-combatants, such as stretcher-bearers, nurses, doctors
chow mein:	a popular American form of a Chinese dish including fried noodles. From the air the land looks hot and moist and made up of chopped-up pieces. The Americans, never good at understanding the Vietnamese, might be expected to treat them as if they were indistinguishable from the Chinese
heading south:	to Australia
heading east:	to the United States
sterile housing:	the antiseptic temporary coffins containing the bodies of the dead within the aircraft
mash ... splendour:	the confusion and physical crushing of their last moments together with the sense of heroism or release from the sordidness of life. MASH is the US army abbreviation of Mobile Army Surgical Hospital, where many of the soldiers would have been taken to die
frozen sunset:	the sunset that has metaphorically overtaken their masters' lives, 'frozen' in the sense that it is final and unchanging
muzzles:	the same word is used of dogs and of rifles
leaves:	another example of Dawe's ability to combine an imaginative metaphor (telegrams like leaves falling from a tree) with a familiar dead metaphor (telegrams as leaves of paper)
spider grief:	personification or emblematic description of grief as a spider, swinging at the heart of a web of relationships that have suffered from the loss of a loved one
too late, too early:	too late to preserve their lives, too early for war to have ended

QUESTIONS:
1. How and why is cold used as a repeated image?
2. How does Dawe suggest the stark ironic contrast between expectations of a hero's homecoming and the actual process?

'One Jump Ahead', p. 96 (*Sometimes Gladness*, 1978, p. 99; *Condolences*, p. 84)

A 1968 poem in free verse about a family of 'drifters' (the title of another 1968 poem on a similar subject). They make a practice of moving from suburb to suburb, renting a house, then stocking it with furniture and electric goods which they agree to buy on hire-purchase (sometimes called 'time-payment' or simply 'credit'), but never actually begin to pay for. Dawe presents the nature and hopes of the man and wife, their attitude to life, and their mode of living. The husband is cunning, with an ability to foresee how his family will wreck a neat rented home. The woman glows with pleasure at the thought of shiny new possessions, as if she were to give birth to a child. Dawe does not condemn the loose sense of morality of the family. What he does is give a clear delineation of the character of the two people and of the attitudes that motivate them.

NOTES AND GLOSSARY:

solicitors: a firm of lawyers which has been asked by the hire-purchase company to begin legal action to seize the goods not paid for or to recover the debt in some other way

robes: the letter hints at action in a court, where legal robes are sometimes worn

Westinghouse: a popular brand of washing machine

trailer: designed to be pulled by a car

clean places: the places where furniture has stood are cleaner than the rest of the house, which has been rarely cleaned

cactuses: succulent pot-plants, apparently belonging to the rented house

Danish: a style of furniture popular in Australia, made of undecorated timber with low backs, of Scandinavian origin

de Luxe: a meaningless advertising description intended to make a product seem more desirable

lounge suite: a set of chairs, usually upholstered and comprising matching two- or three-seaters and single chairs

fridge: refrigerator

estate agent's: a business concerned with renting, buying, and selling houses

bushrangers: thieves who used to live in the Australian bush and rob coaches and banks

His Nibs: used facetiously of someone who considers himself important

barrels: a continuation of the analogy with bushrangers

zinc: widely used in Australia as a protection for iron sheeting against rust. Presumably the dog's teeth come in contact with many substances without being affected

unnameable:	the only appropriate names would be very impolite
pirouettes:	spins around, as in ballet dancing
pressure-cooker:	saucepan with tight-fitting lid that cooks by pressurised steam more quickly than ordinary saucepans
Walton's:	an Australia-wide department store
surety:	security, both personal and financial; ironic in the second sense because the money they guarantee to repay never will be repaid
cubicles ... :	the credit-manager's department where hire-purchase contracts are signed
ten-cents ... :	an annual interest rate of ten per cent
quickens:	springs into life and excitement; a word also used of a pregnant woman when the movements of the foetus can be felt. The tone is satiric, mock-heroic

QUESTIONS:
1. How does Dawe characterise the man and the woman?
2. What evidence is there that the outlook of this family is mostly directed to the future?

'Easy Does It', p. 107 (*Sometimes Gladness*, 1978, p. 41; *Condolences*, p. 76)

A poem in blank verse written when his son was four years of age. It uses the problems of a child learning to talk and being corrected by a parent as a symbol for two ways of looking at the world: the creative and experimental on one side and the rigid and orderly on the other. The first is represented by the child's play with words and toys and by disdainful swans; the second by a museum model, petrification, and trying to feed swans in a man-made park. Dawe is, of course, aware of the danger of himself as a parent falling into the rigidity of the second mode.

NOTES AND GLOSSARY:

title:	a common expression when one needs to be careful not to cause damage while doing a difficult or physically demanding job. The author feels like a workman with a lot of intellectual power at his disposal which he may use in ways that damage the boy on whose mind he is working
above his head:	a pun, because the common expression, 'above his head', meaning beyond his comprehension, here has ceased being a 'dead' metaphor and has come to life with the revival of the literal meaning. The word 'aeroplane' which the boy is trying to say refers to an object that would be, literally, 'above

Immelmanns: his head'. Dawe often brings dead metaphors to life (as does Milton) flying manoeuvres consisting of a half-loop and a half-roll used to gain height and reverse direction. The son uses words so that they dart about in startling ways. The father uses them in thoroughly predictable ways, like a working model in a glass case in a museum

immediate . . . extensible: a parody of advertising language, here ironically applied to a much more important subject, experience of the world; the reverse of a mock-heroic effect because it applies trivial language to a deeply significant subject

petrify . . . gaze: as if the rules of grammar were like a Gorgon, which in Greek mythology could turn an observer to stone. Dawe also envisages another kind of transformation that keeps the observer alive but turns him into a rigidly programmed being who even needs special crusts to feed to swans. This represents the living death of the mechanistic unimaginative life

QUESTIONS:
1. How does Dawe make one kind of attitude to life seem more appealing than the other?
2. How does the second verse-paragraph parallel the first in its patterns of ideas and language?

'Wood-Eye', p. 128 (*Sometimes Gladness*, 1978, p. 140; *Condolences*, pp. 98-9)

A 1970 poem in free verse derived from Dawe's experiences when he was in hospital at an Air Force base in Victoria. The man nicknamed 'Wood-eye' was a patient who came in daily. He suffered from a cancerous growth in one eye, which could have led to his death, but he was full of bubbling wit. Much of it was based on sexual innuendo: everything in the hospital ward, including the nursing-sisters, reminded him of sex.

'Wood-eye' is a name given to him partly because his eyes swivelling about (one unseen) were like wood in which mysterious carved meanings might be seen: his eyes would take on a glint that told his fellow patients that some witty comment suggestive of sex was about to follow. The name also derived from his favourite saying: 'Would I, what!', meaning 'Would I jump at the chance to have sexual intercourse with her? There's no doubt about it!'

Towards the end of the middle verse-paragraph Dawe suggests that behind the banter and camaraderie there was a sombre, fearful person. This mood carries over into the last paragraph, where Dawe speaks of fear of the surgeon's knife and Wood-eye's need 'to grin upon a leaden fate'. The poet here explores his own feelings if he were to know that Wood-eye had been cured. In lines reminiscent in style of Dylan Thomas he expresses the secure knowledge that he would rejoice – there is no doubt about it.

NOTES AND GLOSSARY:

lamb...lion's: a proverbial contrast of meekness and aggression

Calm...pulse: another contrast, between the composure (almost stealth) of the nurse and the excitement of Wood-eye's pulse

libido: sexual urge

red-light: the conventional sign indicating a brothel

last street: one of the first suggestions of Wood-eye's nearness to death. The first such suggestion is 'still unbandaged', indicating that Wood-eye may soon lose his other eye

Gomorrah: a city notorious for its sexual depravity (see the Bible, Genesis, chapters 18–19)

resident specialist: Wood-eye, at least in his imagination, is like a doctor specialising in sexual matters, available at all hours of the day

phallic: associated with the penis

spatula: flat-bladed instrument used for lifting small non-rigid objects

consummation...wished: quotation from Hamlet's soliloquy in Shakespeare's *Hamlet*, III. 1.63–4. Here 'consummation' is given the specific meaning of sexual conclusion

cool: in both the modern American meaning of stylish, elegant, and the older meaning of calm, unruffled

gauze-pad: surgical dressing

totems: objects having ritual significance; here the ritual is the game of sexual innuendo in which the Air Force patients engage with Wood-eye each day

anchorites: hermits, religious recluses who often spent almost their entire life lying down, taking a minimum of food and drink

pennon: as used in medieval times, a long narrow flag or banner

ravaged: tormented

figure...dawn: like a mysterious one-man patrol in jungle warfare

42 · Summaries

nothing...silences: anything he actually said was outweighed or drowned out by the message in what he did not say; in other words what he said in no way conveyed the horror and insecurity that tormented him during the nights when he left the hospital and returned home. 'Music/silences' is an oxymoron, a rhetorical figure containing two terms of contradictory meaning

racing rink: a skating arena, suggestive of the speed and slipperiness of Wood-eye's thoughts about sex

leaden: dull, discouraging

sober skin: Dawe seems to think of himself as a rather dull observer of the hospital wit as he meditated on the mystery of life and the nearness of death, but now he envisages himself as breaking out and flowing over with enthusiasm like juice bursting from grapes as they are made into wine. Sober/wine is another oxymoron, emphasising the great change that would occur in his mood if he learnt of Wood-eye's recovery. The wine image hints at the Christian Mass, a religious service in which wine is used to link the death of Jesus with his love for the world

QUESTIONS:
1. Are the three verse-paragraphs parallel in the order of their thoughts and images?
2. What effects do the various contrasts have in the poem?

'The Museum Attendant', p. 134 (*Sometimes Gladness*, 1978, p. 83; *Condolences*, p. 104)

A free-verse poem of 1970 depicting the hard, factual, demythologising approach of a museum attendant to the weaponry he cleans, cares for, and displays. The involvement, glamour, and fascination of their original users are wiped away and in their place is revealed the evil and destructive 'serpent' of war. The superficial glamorous attraction ('sheen') that children bring to the exhibit of weaponry is also removed, so that they leave the display with some understanding of the real nature of war.

The first three verse-paragraphs describe war as it was fought (or at least depicted) up to the second half of the nineteenth century (when the rifle and machine-gun came into general use), but they are largely eighteenth-century in detail. All three of these paragraphs seem inspired

Summaries · 43

by paintings of heroic battles of the kind popular from the time of the Duke of Marlborough to Napoleon. The fourth paragraph is set in the twentieth century, right up to the time of contemporary children who are drawn to the military section of a large museum. The museum is like life; the military display a major, magnetically attractive part of life. The attendant's unemotional, factual display enables the children to discard their romantic notions about war and to understand what adults are really doing when they engage in it.

NOTES AND GLOSSARY:

moist gaze: the generals (safe from the battle which they observe from hills) are overcome by pride at the achievements of their men or guilt at having sent them to their death

huzzas: shouts of encouragement or excitement such as were used during a battle charge; an old-fashioned word appropriate to an historical military setting

witch-fire: strictly a ball of fire, especially as seen during a storm at sea, but here applied to the effect of an eighteenth-century set-piece battle with muskets firing volleys at the enemy

storming...: the gallant exploits of eighteenth-century armies demand to be recorded in regimental mess-halls (where a group or regiment of soldiers eats when in barracks) and museums. It is as if they were attacking (storming) the walls of these institutions, demanding to be let in with their romantic concept of warfare

mystique: in paintings and picture-books, soldiers in battle are commonly depicted with faces lit up with inspiration, faith, and determination

sabre: curved cavalry sword

broadsword: broad-bladed cutting sword, much used by Scottish troops

French...Scots: recalling the eighteenth- and nineteenth-century wars between Britain and France and the widespread use of Scots troops as mercenaries in European armies in the eighteenth century. Scottish troops were noted for their swearing (including the use of 'bloody' – hence 'red' oaths, with their ironic application to an occupation where blood would literally be spilt)

torpid: sluggish, dormant, like the spirit of warfare which often sleeps but is terrible when roused

44 · Summaries

serpent of light: serpent suggestive of evil and sin; light suggestive of the false glamour and heroism of war. The attendant arranges his display to reveal this true nature of warfare
fills ... empties: war can be the 'cradle' of a civilisation and the destruction of one; soldiers can father individual children or kill them
bites ... poisons: here war is spoken of in terms of its destructiveness, which is like that of a serpent
rapid-fire: like the quick-firing automatic weapons used in the Vietnam War
calibres: diameter of projectiles and bores of guns
Schmeisser ... Sten: designers of weapons of German, Swedish, Japanese and British origin
M 1 ... AK 47: automatic small-arms made in the USA, Belgium, and USSR

QUESTIONS:
1. Make a list of words indicating the romance and the machine-like efficiency of war.
2. How does Dawe make his conventional heroic pictures of war seem slightly ridiculous?

'Weapons Training', p. 147 (*Sometimes Gladness*, 1978, p. 87; *Condolences*, p. 118)

A 1970 dramatic monologue beginning in quatrains of five-stress lines rhyming *a b b a* (the stanza-pattern of *In Memoriam* (1850) by the English poet, Alfred, Lord Tennyson (1809–92)). The strict pattern of rhyme breaks down as the speaker graphically describes an imaginary attack, and is then resumed. The poem closes with a couplet.

The speaker is apparently a sergeant drilling a squad of new recruits in the use of the light machine-gun. Dawe would have been familiar with the circumstances from his own basic training in 1959, but the sergeant's language is up-dated to the time of the Vietnam War in the second half of the 1960s. (The most famous poem of the idiosyncracies of military drill is 'Lessons of the War' (about 1946) by the English poet Henry Reed (1914–). The first of its three sections, 'Naming of Parts', is frequently anthologised.)

The squad is a new intake of recruits. The sergeant has not yet learnt their names so he resorts to gross physical descriptions to intimidate them and ensure that they are attentive. He has a stock of jokes to assert his superiority at the expense of the men, but they are not to be laughed at, for that would disturb discipline. The sergeant is consciously using his military authority, command of rapid-fire language, ridicule, projection of sexual powers, and contempt for the habits of the enemy to instil discipline, attention, fear, and learning into the recruits. He begins with a drill movement ('eyes right'), then summarises an earlier lesson on going down to ground ('cockpit drill'). Presumably he gives the order for the men to go to ground and checks the position in which the weapons are held. At that point he changes his tone of voice and slows down his rapid-fire delivery of words: 'allright now suppose/for the sake of argument...'. He gives a verbal picture of an attack by a new group of Viet Cong ('Charlies') just at the time when the gun will not fire. He tells one recruit to show what action he would take: 'grab and check the magazine'. But the recruit's action is too slow for the sergeant's sense of necessary urgency. He completes the scene he has set by envisaging the death of the recruit, taken by surprise by the enemy. The last few lines are stridently shouted, suggesting tenseness, even panic perhaps, as the sergeant seems to re-live one of his own battlefront experiences. What began as light-hearted verbal play has come round to the seriousness of warfare and the nearness of death.

NOTES AND GLOSSARY:
queer: homosexual (an insult)
cockpit drill: practice at going down to ground in order to fire at the enemy
crown jewels: a metaphor for genitals (because of their value)
little yellows: enemy in South-East Asia described, with racial superiority, by their colour
turning...ignition: metaphor from starting a car applied to the insertion of the penis into the vagina
number-one blockage: the commonest fault in a light machine-gun, when the cartridge fails to pass correctly from the magazine to the barrel
tit: breast
nit: louse egg as found in human hair, used as a form of abuse and derision (sometimes in the form 'nitwit')
tripes: intestines
copped: suffered, received
bloody: common Australian expletive, but here literally true as well

QUESTIONS:
1. What are the ways in which the instructor insults the men in the squad?
2. How does the tone of the instructor modulate between the serious and the comic?

'Teaching the Syllabus', p. 153 (*Sometimes Gladness*, 1978, p. 66)

A poem of 1970 in quatrains with lines mostly of five stresses in a trochaic pattern (that is, a stressed syllable comes before an unstressed one). The chief idea is similar to that in 'Easy Does It', the danger of knowing too much in compartments that are too rigid. Almost every line in the first three stanzas begins with 'Teaching'; it is as if the process of teaching and the fact that something can be taught have overwhelmed all judgment about whether it should be taught. The poet imagines himself as a circus trainer, teaching animals a range of tricks. In the third stanza he moves beyond the circus metaphor to sum up the process he has been describing in different, boldly satiric terms. The last stanza makes the point that teaching tricks can cause natural abilities to wither away, so that – to return to the circus metaphor again – the animals have to be taught their instinctive functions again. Teaching, in other words, Dawe is saying, can be quite misguided, engaged in for its own sake without due consideration of its purpose.

NOTES AND GLOSSARY:
title: the syllabus is thought of as an impersonal set of facts and skills imposed by a bureaucracy on all teachers and students
chimps: chimpanzees
rhumbas (often spelt rumbas): the rhumba is a syncopated dance of Cuban origin adapted for ballroom use in the 1930s
Highland fling: an energetic dance for several couples from the Highlands of Scotland
Tossing . . . dry: a teacher's satiric and bitter view of his function. He feels that what he is doing is as idle as making a wish by tossing coins in a fountain (a common practice in Italy). The fountain (the ability or intellect of the pupil) is not even turned on continuously: it fails to respond – outside help is sought, probably in the form of a school counsellor or psychologist (metaphorically, a plumber). 'Dry' is not merely appropriate to the metaphor of a fountain; it is a common dead metaphor in everyday speech, as in 'dried up' for having nothing further to say, or 'dry as dust' for school lessons. Once again Dawe has brought his own metaphorical inventiveness and common usage together

QUESTIONS:
1. The second stanza has some short lines. Is there anything different

in what the hawks and seals are taught that makes the short lines appropriate?
2. Why do you think Dawe breaks away from the circus metaphor in stanza three? What feeling about the process of teaching does the poet express here?

'Pleasant Sunday Afternoon', p. 161 (*Sometimes Gladness*, 1978, p. 116)

A dramatic monologue in blank verse, written in 1973. An ill-educated man, with an untidy house and unruly children rather like those of 'One Jump Ahead', is visited on a Sunday afternoon by an encyclopaedia salesman. Comedy arises from the incongruity between the knowledge within the encyclopaedia and the crude ignorance of the family, the disparity between the salesman's implied expectations of a sale and the destructive behaviour of the family, and the hint of uneasiness leading to bewilderment and ultimately to ignominious flight while the father continues to chat, blithely unaware of the havoc his family has caused.

The poem begins with little suggestion of the comic farce to follow. The salesman has shown a brochure with its advertising of 'TWENTY-EIGHT MAGNIFICENT FULLY ILLUSTRATED VOLUMES' and, as part of his sales talk, has said that a survey of world knowledge (a 'synopticon' or 'panopticon' perhaps) comes absolutely free if the set of volumes is bought. He makes the disastrous mistake of producing a set of the encyclopaedias and opening it. The man calls his wife ('Eth'), who comes from the stove with greasy hands which she puts on the pages. She returns with a knife that has been left on the stove intending to lift the grease off the page, but instead scorches it. By this time the salesman is trying to retreat, but his polite gestures are ignored by the father, who has become quite interested. One of the children, Stewart, seems to vomit over the pages. Another, Graham, defecates on the floor and uses the encyclopaedia to wipe himself. One child sets about ripping up a volume, which the father tries to put back into the right order. In the end the salesman bolts from the disaster, leaving his ruined set of encyclopaedias behind.

NOTES AND GLOSSARY:
title: the city missions of the Methodist Church in Australia used to run Sunday afternoon functions called 'Pleasant Sunday Afternoons', mixtures of talks by well-known people, music, and religious worship. The title is here ironic, at least from the salesman's point of view

Thingummy-thon: the ill-educated father has not quite heard the unusual title of the summary and index volume (probably a 'synopticon' or 'panopticon'). He assimilates the word to something he does know (for example, a marathon or 'walkathon', a popular means of raising money for charity in Australia), and replaces the distinctive part of the word with 'Thingummy' (commonly used when one has forgotten the right name of something)

nothing ... practically: the man is speaking more truly than he knows. What is presented by the salesman as something 'for nothing' is of course to be well paid for in the set of encyclopaedias. 'Well practically' (that is, *almost* for nothing) is unintentionally ironic

Eth: short for 'Ethel', his wife's name

Black and White Minstrels: a sarcastic comment about his wife's dirty hands and face, based on the popular minstrel show in which white singers blackened their faces to imitate black men and performed a 'minstrel show' (that is, ballads, dances, and comedy routines from the American South)

up to buggery: a vulgar expression suggestive of complete destruction

(italics): the italics are used for emphasis, as the man raises his voice

sticky-tape: clear cellulose tape used for mending or sealing

Tim Tyler: the hero of an American comic strip, *Tim Tyler's Luck*, very popular in Europe and Australia in the 1930s and 1940s. Tyler was a free-lance adventurer always getting into dangerous situations. 'In more trouble than Tim Tyler' was once a common expression

treat: pleasant surprise; used ironically

you won't believe this: unintentionally ironic; the salesman will have little difficulty believing that few visitors subject themselves to this riotous family

QUESTIONS:
1. Like many dramatic monologues, this one assumes some unrecorded replies or comments by the person addressed. Where do you think they occur and what might they have been?
2. The man begins his monologue rather hesitantly. Show how and why he gradually builds up confidence and command of the situation.

'The Privilege', pp. 179-80 (*Sometimes Gladness*, 1978, p. 179)

The most recent poem (written in 1978) in the first edition of *Sometimes Gladness*. This somewhat diffuse piece of free verse is, like several other poems of similar date such as 'Open Invitation' or 'News from Judaea', concerned with limitations on civil liberties in the state of Queensland, where Dawe lives. This poem proceeds by several (largely unconnected) bursts of bitter but witty political comment. It is addressed to residents in other, more liberal, states of Australia, beginning with a plea for concern and for self-congratulation that political affairs are handled better in their states. It ends with an ironic claim that Queenslanders are especially fortunate.

In other states, Dawe begins by saying, commerce and nature can be spoken of together. Skies close like shops; the stars have their peak-hour like traffic. In Queensland, however, even nature seems to be under an unjust rule of law. Police in large numbers are employed to spy on citizens and prevent them from engaging in marches and protest. One might even come to think that laughter was subject to government regulation. The government of Queensland (or at least that part of the coalition representing farming interests) is antipathetic to unions and Aborigines (the black inhabitants of Australia who were dispossessed by white settlers but who still exist in substantial numbers in Queensland). It also keeps a close watch on the school curriculum and has prevented the use of certain text-books and other teaching materials in social science subjects. It has been accused of lavish spending of public money on projects from which cabinet ministers have benefited and two ministers have allegedly received favourable terms from Russian and Japanese business institutions. The poem ends with a suggestion that life (standing for personal and intellectual freedom) is in danger of dying in Queensland.

NOTES AND GLOSSARY:
carbon-monoxide: the chief pollutant from motorcar engines
out on bail: Queensland police, acting on government orders, sometimes arrest hundreds of protesters. Most are let out on bail (that is, released after the payment of a money bond which is forfeited if they do not appear in court). In 1978 Dawe himself was arrested following an 'illegal' civil-liberties march which he led in Toowoomba; he refused bail and spent the night in gaol
self-recognizance: bail when the bond is provided by the person arrested rather than on his or her behalf by someone else
praying-mantis: a green insect which holds up its front legs as if

	praying. The oblique reference is to some Christian clergymen who were arrested for disturbing the peace by singing hymns in a park
special branches:	police are presented as ape-like, swinging from the trees. One of the most detested squads in the police force is the 'Special Branch', which is concerned with political dissent and protest and with crowd control. They appear at demonstrations taking photographs of prominent protesters to add to police files
shoot bank bandits:	many policemen resent being taken from normal duties to provoke or restrain demonstrators. There is some ill-feeling between ordinary policemen in uniform and the specialised squads (such as detectives, or members of the Special Branch)
arms linked:	standard method of crowd control by police
rural obsession:	a reference to domination of the government by farming interests
professional martyrs:	police ill-treatment of leading demonstrators turns them into martyrs for civil liberty
Bylaw 49a:	an imaginary by-law, of course, but much of the police action against demonstrators is based on the commission of offences set out in obscure regulations (that is, by-laws) issued under the Traffic Act
Right to Laugh:	a parody of Right to Life, an organisation (largely made up of Catholics) which campaigns against the liberalisation of abortion law. It is strongly represented in Queensland
Slack's Creek ... Acacia Ridge:	outer suburbs of Brisbane
KuKuKuKu:	'laughing sickness' is the popular name for Kuru, a horrifying fatal disease of the nervous system unique to parts of the Eastern Highlands of Papua New Guinea; one of its early symptoms is uncontrollable nervous laughter. The Kukukuku are one of the peoples living in the area where the disease is prevalent. 'Kukukuku' is also suggestive of the derisory bird-call of the cuckoo with its overtones of madness or folly ('to be cuckoo' is to be at least mildly insane, in everyday speech) and of the right-wing, anti-black, anti-semitic secret society in the United States of America, the Ku Klux Klan
Tweed:	the river marking part of the boundary between Queensland and its neighbouring state, New South Wales

union picket:	a member of a trade union who during a strike attempts to see that no one works in defiance of the strike; a function unpopular with the Queensland government. Dawe's mention of burning such people or Aborigines is, of course, an exaggeration
suttee'd:	suttee is the ritual burning of a widow, a former Hindu custom. Dawe suggests that when the government banned some social science text-books from the classroom (an action similar to medieval book burnings) one or two teachers might have felt like committing suicide on the imaginary funeral pyre of books
bushel:	a measure used particularly for grain and other produce; an appropriate word for a large amount of wasted or misused money when those accused of the action are farmers in government
rouble and yen:	one very senior cabinet minister obtained a very favourable personal loan from a Russian bank; the premier of the state has many Japanese business connections
Europe's yesterday:	one of political repression, likely, says Dawe, to be like Australia's future
we locals:	inhabitants of Queensland
Abel's special privilege:	of being the first human to be killed; see the Bible, Genesis 4:8
Cain:	the first murderer (of his brother Abel). The Queensland premier is fond of quoting from the Bible; here his government is accused of acting as a murderer towards civil rights

QUESTIONS:
1. List the critical points that Dawe makes about the administration of the state of Queensland.
2. How does he exaggerate for satiric effect?

'The Vision Splendid', p. 182

A 1979 satire on the Hon. Johannes Bjelke-Petersen, Premier of Queensland. It is in the form of a dramatic monologue, but the speaker addresses himself, as in a soliloquy. Dawe intends us to recall the self-righteous Pharisee in the Bible (see St Luke 18:10–12) who went into the temple and 'prayed thus with himself, God I thank thee, that I am not as other men are, extortioners, unjust, adulterers, or even as this publican'. To Dawe, the Premier is a hypocrite who makes a profession of Christian piety but exhibits intolerance, bigotry, uncharitableness, and self-interest. He has him use a number of expressions from the Bible, including sayings of Jesus, to suggest that he regards himself as godlike and, like Jesus, reviled by the wicked.

Mr Bjelke-Petersen was fifty-seven when he rather improbably became Premier of Queensland in 1968. He has ruled for a record term of over seventeen years. Dawe refers to a number of incidents and characteristics in his career: his farming background, belief in youth groups (particularly church ones as a means of producing docile citizens), the building of a twenty-three-storey parliamentary annexe, with his own suite on the top floor, his domination of the legislative assembly, his widespread business investments, his stumbling over his words when excited, his detestation of university students and protesters, and his contempt for the parliamentary Opposition.

NOTES AND GLOSSARY:

title: reminiscent of a phrase in a well-known Australian poem, 'Clancy of the Overflow', by A.B. Paterson (1864–1941): 'the vision splendid of the sunlit plains extended'. 'The vision splendid' was earlier used by the English poet William Wordsworth (1770–1850) in his 'Ode: Intimations of Immortality'

a generation of vipers: an echo of the words of Jesus, 'O generation of vipers, who hath warned you to flee from the wrath to come?' (St Matthew 3:7; 23:33). Compare the last line of the poem

eyrie: eagle's nest, usually built in an inaccessible spot on high ground

smokes...plain: Mr Bjelke-Petersen was proud of having cleared vast tracts of land in Queensland for agriculture

mica-points: mica consists of mineral crystals including aluminium; Mr Bjelke-Petersen was attacked in 1970 because he gained for his wife and for members of his Cabinet shares in the multi-national aluminium company, Comalco, at less than the market price

run...stubble: reminiscent of words used about 'the souls of the righteous' in *The Wisdom of Solomon* (in the biblical Apocrypha) 3:7: 'they shall shine, and run to and fro like sparks among the stubble'

O Jerusalem: the words of Jesus when he wept over Jerusalem, 'thou that killest the prophets' (St Matthew 23:37)

dividends of your purpose: the allusion is to Mr Bjelke-Petersen's interest in share-dealings and his Protestant belief that God financially rewards those who are true to him

entrap: Mr Bjelke-Petersen has often faced hostile news-conferences

Pharisee: on several occasions the orthodox Jewish party of the Pharisees sent representatives to Jesus to try to trap him into a statement that was heretical or treasonable; he always evaded the trap by turning the question aside. See the Bible, for example, St Matthew 22:15–22.

Mr Bjelke-Petersen is notorious for answering the question he wants to be asked, not the one actually asked by reporters

valley of decision: a biblical phrase (from Joel 3:14) but Dawe combines this solemn phrase with the accoutrements of modern politics, the airport lounge, and the parliamentary suite of rooms. There is a pun on 'lounge suite', the common Australian term for a set of matching padded chairs and couches

rabble in Shiloh Drive: a reference to civil-liberties marches by demonstrators from the University of Queensland; Sir Fred Schonell Drive (named after a former Vice-Chancellor) is the main road leading from the University towards the city of Brisbane. The similar-sounding Shiloh was a sacred Jewish town in ancient Palestine

King David Square: King George Square is the main city square in Brisbane, where demonstrations were held (often after a march from the University); Mr Bjelke-Petersen is represented as thinking of it in terms of the biblical King David

Skyhooks: a very successful pop-music group, the name being used here partly because of its heavenly suggestion, partly because the group did record a song, 'Over the Border', dealing largely with the Premier

rightful inheritance: the language suggests the children of Israel entering the Promised Land

New South Wales: the neighbouring state to Queensland; it is normally governed by the Labour Party, which is the Opposition in Queensland. In the Skyhooks' song, the singer escapes 'over the border Down in New South Wales'

QUESTIONS:
1. Does the speaker seem both naive and self-confident?
2. Do the speaker's pretentious language and imagery disguise an essentially small-minded ambition?

'The Wholly Innocent', p. 190

For this 1980 poem Dawe has chosen ballad metre, perhaps because it was often used by the English Romantic poets William Blake (1757–1827) and Wordsworth in their poems about children. Dawe's subject is abortion, to which, in accordance with Catholic moral principles, he is opposed. The poem is a lament spoken by the aborted foetus. The diction, with its relative simplicity and use of many well-worn rhymes, is like that of Blake or Wordsworth or, most especially, the nineteenth-century American poet Emily Dickinson (1830–86). Emily Dickinson often has the same impish humour when dealing with major moral problems as Dawe. Her poems such as 'I never hear the word "escape"' (with its mention of prison bars), 'I taste a liquor never brewed', 'I never felt at home below', 'I never saw a moor', and 'I never hear that one is dead' have many resemblances in thought and diction to 'The Wholly Innocent'. Blake's 'Infant joy' (beginning 'I have no name') also offers some parallels.

The foetus condemns the process of abortion (and hence wins sympathy for opposition to abortion) on the grounds that the opportunities of a human life were lost, the foetus had no say in the process, trust was betrayed, and, logically extended, the process would eliminate the whole human race.

NOTES AND GLOSSARY:
sovereign: supreme (normally used in a favourable sense, but here rather oddly attached to 'care')
bucket: the suggestion is that there is something sordid and dirty about the operation aborting the foetus
'genocide': the killing of a whole nation or ethnic group, here extended to the whole of humanity
bloody space: the womb after the operation, when the foetus has been removed (and thus killed)
shambles: originally a slaughter-house; Dawe revives the original, obsolete meaning for emotive effect. He suggests that the use of abortion has spread across the world
ZPG: zero population growth, a suggested aim to contain the growth of the world's population

QUESTIONS:
1. Do you consider the argument offered by the aborted foetus to be fair? What means does the poet use to make the argument persuasive?
2. Is the last line of each stanza especially forceful?

'The Swimming Pool', p. 196

A 1980 poem in blank verse with some hints of partial rhyme. Dawe presents himself and his family as showing 'supreme incompetence' at the annual task of re-erecting an above-ground swimming pool at the beginning of summer. It seems an alien object in an alien landscape, where the rock has been only roughly cut away to provide a not quite level site. It is made of polyvinyl chloride (PVC) sheeting held together by a galvanised iron ('galvabond') frame. Overnight it collects insects. In the morning the Dawe family worry over the irregular working of the pump that filters the water and look earnestly for any trace of algae, the growth on the walls that shows too little of the chemical purifier (brand-named hydrophane) has been added to the water.

The poem suggests the romantic ideals implicit in setting up a pool in the garden: the sense of recreating the sea; of establishing one's mastery over a wayward piece of engineering; of providing, with the connivance of nature, a pastime enjoyed by the family; and of setting the demands of duty aside.

NOTES AND GLOSSARY:
dedication: Mark Macleod is a poet and lecturer who wrote an MA thesis on Dawe's work
three indifferent seasons: the summer during the last three years has not been particularly good for swimming
mare nostrum: (*Latin*) our sea
con: short for confidence trick
sucker: deceive
give the forks to: perhaps make a rude sign by two fingers extended upward like the prongs of a fork

QUESTIONS:
1. Contrast the evidence of incompetence with the evidence of attempts to be efficient and businesslike about the pool.
2. How does Dawe indicate, through the language of the last three lines, that the family's hopes are impossible to realise?

Part 3

Commentary

Major qualities

Bruce Dawe writes poetry that is Australian, intelligible, popular, witty, and morally aware. Although he often uses satire, he is unlike most satirists in so far as he seeks to reconcile rather than divide. A great deal of his poetic effort has, indeed, gone into drawing opposites together. The language he uses brings together international English and Australian usages, the poetic and prosaic, the ordinary man's language and the scholar's. Poetry for him is about the concerns that surround and oppress the ordinary person; and its basic texture is not the hieratic language of an educated élite but the demotic spoken language heard every day in the city and suburban streets of Australia. Yet he neither writes down to some notion of an ill-educated mass nor underestimates the comprehension of his audience. He uses the common style for uncommonly inventive and imaginative linguistic constructions. In his subjects, he brings the drabness, frustration, and bewilderment of the city and the suburbs into a poetic world of reference that includes biblical episodes, European and Asian history, American films, and television commercials. He does not mock the common man and his interests; he understands them, sympathises with them, and sets them in a context where they have equal status with such traditional subjects as love, life, and death.

Australian in language

Dawe's poetry of the 1950s is less original and enterprising than his later work. It is fairly rigid in poetic shape, its syntax has the occasional inversions of standard word-order that are tolerated in conventional poetry, and its choice of language is self-consciously polysyllabic. By the early 1960s these traces of awkwardness had almost disappeared. By then Dawe was prepared to trust the vast fund of common speech that he had stored up during his adolescent and working years and had added to by avid reading of popular American fiction. What his poetry gained – and what was an original contribution to Australian literature – was the unselfconscious use of spoken language as a basic poetic language. That does not mean that he simply transferred pieces of conversation overheard in the street or the bus into his poems. It means that the order of the words and many of the words themselves were derived from common speech and not from a self-perpetuating literary tradition. An earlier, and at one time very popular, comic Australian poet, C.J. Dennis (1876–1938), had tried to make use of Australian slang, but his success was limited by the confusion of literary cockney with actual Australian slang and by setting slang terms in a conventional poetic word order and stanza form. When Dennis's Melbourne larrikin (a rowdy, crude youth) takes his respectable girl-friend to see *Romeo and Juliet*, his impression of Romeo's fight with Tybalt is as follows:

> Quite natchril, Romeo gits wet as 'ell.
> 'It's me or you!' 'e 'owls, and wiv a yell,
> Plunks Tyball through the gizzard wiv 'is sword,
> 'Ow I ongcored!
> 'Put in the boot!' I sez. 'Put in the boot!'
> "Ush' sez Doreen . . . 'Shame!' sez some silly coot.

The humour here arises largely from the artificiality of the scene. Dawe's version of life in the city and suburbs is, however, realistic rather than burlesque. He writes with a naturalness that develops the oral syntax already being used by some of his older Australian contemporaries such as Douglas Stewart (*b.* 1913) and Judith Wright (*b.* 1915), and extends it to include the ordinary diction of the working class. In drama his achievement is paralleled by the enormously successful *Summer of the Seventeenth Doll* by Ray Lawler (*b.* 1921), first produced in 1955.

View of life

Dawe's view of life is that it is puzzling and fragmentary; that it is possible to be honourable and good, but hardly heroic; that most people are confused and vulnerable; that virtues such as endurance, resilience, and compassion are to be admired; and that the nearness of disappointment, failure, and death justifies a melancholy outlook. If that seems a depressing view of life, it has to be remembered that Dawe is also a very funny writer. It is not uncommon in general for comedy to end in pathos or despair, but that is not Dawe's way. His comic poems, when they deal with solemn matters, merely suggest despair as one possibility. There is always the other possibility of some encouraging new development or some happy future. His view of life as fragmentary makes it impossible for him to believe that the fragments suddenly end up in one pile of tragedy or happiness. He told Craig McGregor, who interviewed him for *In the Making*, that 'The world is a brutal, mysterious, beautiful, inexplicable affair; I'm glad to get this ambivalence in my poetry'. In seeking to explain himself for Ian Hansen's *Bruce Dawe: The Man Down the Street* he said that he saw life 'as I guess most people do, as confusing, bloody, tremendous, meaningful, sad, hilarious, deadly and quite unique. And I find it therefore always just beyond where the typewriter keys are hitting this moment' (p. 50). And a few years later he told Roger McDonald: 'I don't see that the world is the kind of place that you can develop very tightly meshed systems of thought about as a writer' (*Australian Writers on Tape*, 1973).

Dawe's many poems about social and political problems do not, therefore, offer ideological alternatives to present circumstances. What he is concerned to point out is injustice, callousness, self-interest, and the neglect of basic human needs. His sympathy is instinctively with 'the little man' (the 'bottom-dog' as he once called him) – the person whose life is constrained, distorted, and confused by the operation of institutions. Dawe has a characteristic Australian distrust and dislike of impersonal organisations and the people who head them. He fears that they are machines for injustice, obscurantism, and oppression. Where his satiric attacks are directed against individuals it is because he believes they have undergone the inevitable hardening and depersonalisation involved in political (or ecclesiastical) leadership – what he calls 'the poison of office' in 'Reverie of a Swimmer' (p. 106).

A satirical writer rather than a writer of satires?

Dawe is often spoken of as if he were largely a satirist but this is to mistake both the nature of satire and the mood of his poems. Satire is a form of literary attack on human folly and vice that ridicules its object and also expounds a moral principle as a basis for the attack or holds up an ideal mode of conduct as a contrast to what it attacks. Dawe certainly has written some poems that fit this definition. 'Condolences' contains a gentle satire of sentimental women cooing over a baby; 'Teaching the Syllabus' a rather more pointed satire of the institutionalisation of education; and 'The Privilege' a very damaging (but still good-humoured) satire of the government of Queensland. But in many other poems Dawe takes the detached, objective position of the satirist and then proceeds to sympathise with his subject. Instead of mocking, he explains and justifies the people he writes about. 'Weapons Training' may be a parody (an amusing exaggeration) of a drill instructor, but it is not a satire of the man. At the end of the poem we recognise that in the most important thing of all, the confrontation with the nearness of death, he is right. He is in no way being criticised by the author for his view of the mutability of life. In 'Pleasant Sunday Afternoon' there is no such moral agreement between speaker and reader at the end, but there is no moral condemnation of the speaker either. We are not meant to approve of what the speaker, his wife, the children, or the encyclopaedia salesman do, but we are not meant to disapprove of them either. The reader may feel some sympathy for the salesman at the end, but does not feel that there has been an adverse moral judgment on the family. Life is just amusing or pathetic in this way; moral judgment is irrelevant.

The distinction made between satire and sympathetic exposure is not always well understood. Another Australian poet, James McAuley, in reviewing *An Eye for a Tooth*, criticised Dawe for being morally superior in 'The Not-So-Good-Earth' when, according to McAuley, he had no right to be. Now moral superiority is a hallmark of satire, and McAuley makes it quite clear that he thinks Dawe is writing satire and that his moral basis for condemnation is wrong. But it seems that McAuley has mistaken the tone and genre of 'The-Not-So-Good-Earth'. It is neither condemnatory nor, as a whole, satirical. There is some implied satire about lack of comprehension: it is directed towards both the family watching the film and the West watching the East. But the family is not judged to be morally inferior, stupid, or inhumane. They are sympathetic to the Chinese people's struggle for food and their mild impatience with the unrelieved stoicism of the characters can be seen as a criticism of the film for being unrealistic rather than of them for lacking compassion. The poem raises a number of questions (despite its sometimes burlesque humour), but it does so with humanity and understanding rather than with satire. Dawe is satirical when he is campaigning against a specific abuse; when he is seeking to understand a general problem he normally uses only the lightest touches of satire. As he says in a 1967 poem, 'Swamped, or: The Reason for the Lack of Satirical Poetry', satire is too easy; it is like a man shooting ducks when there are so many that it is impossible to miss.

The upside-down view

Satire is, then, too inexact a term to apply to much of Dawe's work. What he often does is look at things from the opposite end to the conventional in a kind of quixotic inversion not dissimilar to the method of the Anglo-Irish dramatist George Bernard Shaw (1856–1950). In 'The Machine' he envisages the possibility of an imaginary machine thinking about the human beings who have invented it; in 'Just a Dugong at Twilight' (one of his pieces of light verse written for *The Toowoomba Chronicle*) he writes about gorillas in a zoo watching television programmes of human motor-racing. This humorous inversion of the normal order is perhaps an extreme form of a more general mode of thinking, that is, the viewing of one thing in terms of another with which it would not normally be associated or the overlaying of one system of language and values by another. Dawe told Roger McDonald that

> the poet has to be indirect, he has to use – often make – a great deal of stress on metaphor to make particular points he wants to make. Personally I often work from one or two images and elaborate on these, because the associations flowing from these I hope will be enough to cover quite a lot of territory.
>
> *(Australian Writers on Tape)*

This provides a good clue to Dawe's method in many poems. It is also a clue to the source of much of his humour: it often arises when the two sides of the metaphor, or the two worlds of discourse that are superimposed, are so incongruous that we are surprised and amused. It is often the case that the world of discourse chosen as a metaphoric description of another world of discourse is noticeably more elevated or less elevated than what it is describing. If it is less elevated we might call it reversed mock-heroic or, perhaps, mock-mundane.

Mock-heroic and mock-mundane

In general, mock-heroic, exemplified in such works as Alexander Pope's (1688–1744) *The Rape of the Lock* (1712 and 1714), uses the diction, gesture, syntax, and mood appropriate to the celebration of great heroic incidents and characters and applies them to matters and characters that are essentially trivial. Its purpose is to re-establish a true scale of values; to show that incidents and characters puffed up with self-importance and solemnity are really unimportant and may be objects of amusement. The effect of the mock-heroic is, however, sometimes almost the reverse of the intention. The glamour and romance applied to the trivial matter may in part suggest that there is something epic or grand or noble in it. This partial reverse effect is a major element in Bruce Dawe's use of the mock-heroic. In 'Free-Will Offering', for instance, Dawe uses the language of the romantic address to a loved one, but instead of talking about roses, carpets of grass, and captivating bird-song, he talks about the realities of life in the city: newspapers and milk being delivered, smoke billowing from factory chimneys, babies crying in maternity hospitals, grass growing through asphalt, and an oily, dirty river. The effect is not to suggest that love in these circumstances is trivial or that the cityscape is drab and ugly. It is to suggest that love can exist equally well in such actual surroundings as in the idealised setting of romantic love poetry. Dawe's mock-heroic is, then, of a special kind. It is yet another example of his sympathetic unifying concept of the world, his ability to bring together material from different worlds of discourse and to find merit in all of it.

Even when Dawe uses a mode that is formally mock-heroic, then, he is edging towards the reverse of mock-heroic. It is the full reverse of mock-heroic, the mock-mundane, where he uses humble, commonplace language to talk about matters of great importance, that is one of the major characteristics of his work. In 'Enter Without So Much As Knocking' he talks about life and death in terms of television, street signs, aggressive car driving, drive-in movies, hard-boiled talk, and the cosmetics of the undertaking trade. The purpose is not to trivialise the subject, but once again to show that there is no real moral or aesthetic distinction to be made between the high and the low, the significant and the insignificant, the eternal and the transitory. All are worth considering; all occupy the one world; each interacts with the others.

An all-embracing view

In some poems it is impossible to use terms such as mock-heroic or mock-mundane with any significance because the two modes are intertwined. In 'Homecoming', for instance, the repeated rhetorical pattern ('they're bringing them home') is the fabric of heroic celebration. But some of the details, the green plastic bags, the deep-freeze lockers, the observations on the variety of hair and, most of all, the description of the appearance of the Mekong Delta as a 'steaming *chow mein*', are what would normally be considered trivial and mundane. The purpose is not to mock the heroic quality or to inflate the mundane, but to suggest that such distinctions make no practical sense. Life simply is a mixture of them all. One might even see Dawe's point of view as somewhat analogous to that of the dramatic form tragi-comedy, or find resemblances to it in the work of Lord Byron and E.E. Cummings, two poets who, like Dawe, had an amused disrespect for pretensions, self-righteousness, and self-importance. Like Byron (1788–1824) and Cummings (1894–1962) (and many writers of tragi-comedies), Dawe balances the comedy and the tragedy, the ludicrousness and the solemnity of life. Even his manner of reading his poems – and he reads them superbly – balances the tone of the voice of the larrikin and the preacher. Much of the dialogue will be read in the pronunciation and intonation patterns that you will hear on any Australian street corner, but as the poem develops Dawe often falls into a ritualistic intonation pattern characteristic of preachers, and he often reads the last line in an exaggerated rising-falling-rising pattern much used by clergymen at the end of sermons and blessings. Dawe's poems do, of course, often come to epigrammatic, sardonic, or even melodramatic endings, for which this kind of reading is appropriate. (The abrupt or shocking ending is, incidentally, a feature of many mystery or adventure stories of the kind that Dawe read voraciously.)

QUESTIONS:
1. Consider one of Dawe's poems and show how choice of language includes both the elevated and the mundane.
2. Look at the endings of a few of Dawe's poems and consider whether they are abrupt, shocking, or epigrammatic.

Revitalisation of ordinary language

One of the specific ways in which Dawe is able to present a diverse, all-inclusive, but non-hierarchical view of the world is by bringing together his imaginative and inventive use of language with commonplace language that was once inventive but has now become stereotyped. In 'Easy Does It' he bring to life the dead metaphor, 'above one's head', used as a synonym for something being too difficult for comprehension. Dawe applies it to his son, trying to say 'aeroplane', an object that would be literally above his head. In 'Teaching the Syllabus' he revivifies the dead metaphor by which we say that a school subject is 'dry'. In 'Homecoming' he reanimates the dead metaphor for a 'leaf' of paper. In 'Getting it Together' he makes literal, in an uproarious way, the popular saying that forms the title. Dawe, in other words, is alert to the value inherent but unacknowledged not just in ordinary human beings and activities but also in ordinary words and dead metaphors that seem to most people to have lost all capacity for vividness.

Subjects

A few years ago, Dawe said that 'to celebrate the commonplace without merely rephrasing existing stereotypes, is, I believe, a viable role for the poet'*. He has always emphasised the need to write about and for the ordinary person. For him poetry should not be an arcane mystery, but something that touches and becomes part of everyday life. But it should not merely reflect life: it should analyse it and draw attention to social problems. In 'Recent Trends in Australian Poetry', a lecture delivered in 1964, he said he meant 'such issues as graft and corruption in government, business and industry, spiritual wickedness in high places. I mean the never-ending tussle of State versus the individual, no matter how good the State or civic-minded the individual. I mean that tremendous fact of migration [to Australia].'† In this lecture he went on to talk about the need for poets to speak for those who, through lack of education or opportunity, could not speak for themselves, for the kind of people who were likely to be oppressed by and alienated from an

---
* 'Australian Poets in Profile: I: Bruce Dawe', *Southerly*, 39, No. 3 (1979), p. 241.
† *Twentieth Century*, 19, No. 1 (1964), 59; reprinted in Basil Shaw, *Times and Seasons*, Cheshire, Melbourne, 1974, p. 64.

uncaring society. It is not surprising, then, that many of the characters in Dawe's poems, whether they are dramatic monologues or narratives, are what he calls 'bottom-dogs' or what are often called in Australian speech 'battlers'. Down-and-outs, beggars, itinerants, workers, Aboriginal Australians, ordinary soldiers, children, adolescents, old people, and those who have suffered loss or an accident are the commonly recurring characters in Dawe's work. They are people who are vulnerable and easily hurt, and Dawe has an instinctive sympathy with them. Their injuries and tragedies are documented from a point of view that can feel their injury but stand just far enough away from it to undertake successfully the task of recording it without overstating or sentimentalising it. Dawe is a bystander, helpless in so far as he cannot enter the tragedy or avert it, but helpful in so far as he can record it and reveal its nature to others.

QUESTIONS:
1. Find examples of Dawe's sympathy with disadvantaged people.
2. Does Dawe hold anyone to blame for the plight of such people?

Political satire

His sense of injustice is also directed, chiefly through satire, to the institutions and office-bearers responsible for it. They are seen often as inhumane, insensitive, self-interested, and destructive. Some of the poems directed against the Premier of Queensland, the Hon. Johannes Bjelke-Petersen, have been particularly vicious. In one poem, 'Greetings from the Underworld', published in the weekend edition of a daily newspaper (*The Weekend Australian*, 17–18 June 1978), he refers to Mr Bjelke-Petersen's racial policies, logic, and commercial dealings as worthy of the German Nazi leaders, Hitler, Himmler, Eichmann, Bormann, and Goering. In a much earlier poem, 'ICI Building', he refers to a corporate 'swindle of gargantuan proportions', symbolised by the disintegration of the panes of glass enclosing a new building (occupied by Imperial Chemical Industries) in Melbourne. In 'At Mass' he directs satiric barbs at the Catholic Church in Australia because of its businesslike approach and its intolerance of emotional honesty.

Elegiac tone

These, then, are the people and the institutions he writes about. In more general terms, his subjects are the nature of experience, the significance of life, the passage of time and the passing of youth, and the constant nearness of death. The fear of not understanding what life is supposed to be about and the haunting sense of mortality often give Dawe's poetry, amid its irreverent wit, a rather melancholy tone. A sense of man being both absurd and tragic, of life being frustratingly imperfect, entwines itself with a sense of lost friendships and lost opportunities to produce an elegiac tone. 'Enter Without So Much As Knocking' suggests that the world is a poorer place for losing even such an aggressive, tough-talking, self-opinionated person as Alice's husband. 'Abandonment of Autos' directs a similar feeling of loss not to human beings but to discarded motorcars. 'Accident and Ambulance Siren' offers a more general instance of the same feeling and applies it fearfully to everyone who is aware of 'that voice from the future at whose insistent summons /we are all speeding'. '"Ghost Wanted; Young, Willing"' is an early instance of Dawe's expression of the louring of death, expressed this time with macabre humour. Some poems are elegies for particular people: 'My Mother in Her Latter Years', 'Going', 'Heat-Wave', 'Wood-Eye', and 'A Victorian Hangman Tells His Love', for instance. Many of these poems are highly emotive, though they are rarely sentimental. While Dawe has no compunction about shocking the reader with vulgarity or bad taste, he almost always controls his sentiment by humour, tough language, or repeated rhetorical devices.

Popularity

Condolences of the Season and *Sometimes Gladness* have been major publishing successes in Australia, selling in their tens of thousands. Apart from the Aboriginal writer Kath Walker (*b*. 1920), no Australian poet has had such popular success since before the first world war, and no poet has ever attracted such a wide range of admirers, from school students to ordinary working people to readers of difficult modern poetry. The reasons are to be sought in Dawe's use of vernacular diction and syntax; his ability to handle a short story or genuinely dramatic monologue in verse; his portrayal of characteristically Australian types, especially the dead-beat, the itinerant, the battler, and the disadvantaged person; his disrespect for authority; his appeal to basic human emotions such as love, fear of death, relief, admiration, and amusement; his ability to operate a wide range of witty and humorous devices; and his ability unselfconsciously to identify with the ordinary person. His poetry is, of course, neither always easy to understand nor always designed for popular appeal. His irony and sarcasm, his wide range of references, his espousal of political judgment in the wider rather than the narrower party sense, his strong moral convictions, and his omnipresent sense of spirituality might have been hindrances to popularity. In fact, however, he is much sought after as a public reader of his poetry and his poetry continues to outsell that of all his contemporaries.

Humour

Dawe is the most amusing poet Australia has produced. His humour arises from attitude, comic invention of plot, the overlaying of images, a good ear for language, and sheer verbal dexterity. His attitude to the situations of life is frequently unorthodox: he is able to reflect on how things might look from the other side – how gorillas might view human beings, for instance. His plots are often outrageously funny because they combine incongruity or irreverence with a masterly dramatic sense. Dad tripping over the television lead or an encyclopaedia salesman having his wares torn to pieces by an undisciplined family are the stuff of burlesque. Dawe's ability to overlay images by speaking of life and death in terms drawn from television, films, cars, and suburban life is another rich source of humour. So too is his excellent ear for commonplace language, which the reader comes upon with a shock of recognition. His verbal dexterity may consist of the fusion of the commonplace with the recondite, masterly control of polysyllabic humour, or outrageous punning. Examples of all of these usages should be easy to find, but you might consider, particularly, the brilliant double pun in 'Credo'. After a comic description of false teeth flying out of the window of a car and lodging in the tyre of a car going the other way, he says that they ended up 'biting their way macademically over Princes Bridge'. In other words, they were biting the macadamised surface of the road as if they were biting a macadamia nut (a particularly hard Australian nut).

Criticisms

Despite his popularity, Dawe has been criticised, particularly by academic reviewers, for what are considered faults in his poetry. The following list covers the main points made against him, and you should consider to what extent you agree with each one:

1. His material is too trite, undignified, or vulgar for poetry.
2. The satire is unfair, ill-considered, and over-emotional.
3. His idiom lacks uniformity and its tone wobbles.
4. His outlook is intellectually light-weight and he arrives at his conclusions too glibly.
5. He is too negative and dismissive.
6. His tone is too self-satisfied, smug, and self-consciously clever.
7. His is too pessimistic, melancholy, and obsessed with death.
8. He writes too much in the voice of the male tough-guy.
9. His religious stance is always assumed, never justified.
10. He tries to be tough, flippant, and sentimental all at once or in regard to the same scene.

Conclusion

The major feature of Dawe's work is probably the comprehensiveness of its outlook. Dawe is able to assimilate into a single poem laughter and tragedy, brutality and tenderness, vulgarity and reverence, simplicity and subtlety. It is poetry of stoic acceptance not judgment, sympathy not condemnation. Human life is puzzling and melancholy, but also full of surprise and excitement. One of the best of his many aphoristic comments on life is that

> We are not comfortable here, but find that it pays
> To accept the fact that our present chances of winning
> Are not very great. Here we are. Here we will end our days.
>
> ('For the Duration')

Part 4
Hints for study

General approach
1. Try to think yourself into Dawe's mind and frame of reference. The earlier sections of these notes will give you a good deal of help, but anything you can find out elsewhere about Australia in the last thirty years, American films and television, life in suburbs, the Catholic religion, and the Vietnam war will be useful.
2. Understand what Dawe is saying before you venture to criticise it.
3. Remember that disagreement about an article of faith or a political attitude is not literary criticism. You may not share Dawe's beliefs about the futility of war, the ordinariness of life, the corrupt practices of governments and large corporations, the religious instinct, or the horror of capital punishment, but what you have to ask is: Does the poet present his point of view in a way that is credible? Is the point of view appropriate to the scene and characters described? Is it consistent with the facts presented? How has he tried to persuade the reader that the attitude is reasonable and acceptable?
4. If possible, try to gain access for reference purposes to a good modern English dictionary that includes Australian usage. The best is *The Macquarie Dictionary*, Macquarie Library, Sydney, 1981, with its various abridgments.
    Other useful dictionaries include *Collins English Dictionary* (Australian Edition), *The Australian Pocket Oxford Dictionary*, and the *Heinemann Australian Dictionary*. You may also gain help from *A Dictionary of Australian Colloquialisms* by G.A. Wilkes, Sydney University Press, Sydney, 1978, and *Australian Folklore: A Dictionary of Lore, Legends and Popular Allusions* by Bill Wannan, Lansdowne, Sydney, 1970.
5. Read as much of Dawe's work as you can. Poems outside those set for class study will often provide useful clues about his attitudes and methods.
6. Try to gain a very clear impression of each poem you have studied. You may even be able to remember certain significant lines and phrases. Then you will be well equipped to answer questions.

7. Prepare yourself for two main kinds of question:
   (*a*) where you are given a poem or a passage from a poem and asked to write about its qualities and perhaps also how it is characteristic of Dawe's work and how it relates to other poems by him. You should be prepared to discuss the ideas, attitudes, and feelings of the poem and how they are expressed through its form and style.
   (*b*) where you are asked to write about some theme or characteristic of Dawe's poetry in relation to a small number of poems either selected for you or left to your own choice. You will often be given a statement of opinion and asked whether you think it is true or appropriate. In your answer you need to marshal your evidence like a lawyer or debater in an attempt to establish the rightness or likelihood of the conclusion you want to arrive at.
   The following examples of questions have been set in the form discussed above as (*b*). Many of them could, however, be applied in detail to a single poem.
8. Do not hesitate to disagree with statements or theories expressed in questions if you think that the evidence of the poems can be used to disprove them.

Some areas for study

City and suburbs

1. Dawe suggests that there is a solidity of ordinariness in the suburbs which should not be despised. Discuss this feature in two or three of Dawe's poems. (You might consider 'Free-Will Offering', 'The Frog Plague', 'Life-Cycle', 'Drifters', 'Suburban Lovers', 'The Rock-Throwers', 'Homo Suburbiensis'. 'Credo', 'In Praise of Second-Hand Paperbacks', 'The Swimming Pool'.)
2. James McAuley spoke of Dawe's 'urban and technological vocabulary'. Discuss this feature in two or three of Dawe's poems and show how it is used for humour and satire. (You might consider 'Enter Without So Much as Knocking', 'Abandonment of Autos', 'ICI Building', 'One Jump Ahead', 'The Museum Attendant', 'Open Invitation', 'Around El Salvador'.)

Anti-war poems

1. 'The horror of death is always evident in Dawe's poems about war.' ('Homecoming', 'The Museum Attendant', 'Vietnam Postscript, 1975', 'Turn Again Home', 'Around El Salvador'.)

Political satire

Satire: an attack on folly and vice using such devices as comic exaggeration and irony (which involves a gap between what is stated and what is meant); it assumes a moral justification for the attack and often suggests a moral ideal.

1. 'Dawe is contemptuous of politicians.' ('Only the Beards Are Different', 'Pigeons Also Are a Way of Life', 'Demons', 'Open Invitation', 'News from Judaea', 'The Privilege', 'The Vision Splendid'.)
2. 'Dawe is too sympathetic to the characters he writes about, too aware of their human uniqueness, to be a bitter satirist.' ('Only the Beards Are Different', 'Pigeons Also Are a Way of Life', 'Demons', 'Open Invitation', 'News from Judaea', 'The Privilege', 'The Vision Splendid'.)

Superimposition of images

1. 'A great deal of Dawe's humour arises from his method of speaking of one world of discourse in terms of another.' (This is such a common technique that you should find your own examples.)
2. Consider the effects of writing about love *or* death *or* religion in terms of such features of contemporary life as films, television, advertising, and popular literature.
3. What do you understand by mock-heroic and mock-mundane (see Part 3: Commentary), and how are they used in Bruce Dawe's work? ('"Ghost Wanted: Young, Willing"', 'Enter Without So Much As Knocking', 'Dogs in the Morning Light', 'Pigeons Also Are a Way of Life', 'And a Good Friday Was Had By All', 'Free-Will Offering', 'For the Duration', 'A Victorian Hangman Tells His Love', 'Open Invitation', 'Life-Cycle', 'Beatitudes', 'Homecoming', 'Suburban Lovers', 'Teaching the Syllabus', 'The Corn Flake', 'The Vision Splendid', 'Quiet Night at the Cosmos', 'Planning a Service'.)

Elegiac mood

Elegy: a poem lamenting the death of a particular person or, more generally, expressing a sense of loss, deprivation, mutability, and the desire for divine consolation.

1. Dawe said that elegies were in part to 'celebrate the love of the elegist for the subject of the elegy'. Choose two of the following

poems and show whether this statement is true or not: 'Soliloquy for One Dead', 'Enter Without So Much As Knocking', 'And a Good Friday Was Had by All', 'The Head Next to Mine on the Pillow', 'My Mother in Her Latter Years', 'Elegy for Drowned Children', 'A Victorian Hangman Tells His Love', 'Katrina', 'Homecoming', 'At Shagger's Funeral', 'Reverie of a Swimmer', 'Wood-Eye', 'Widower', 'Going', 'Heat-Wave', 'Returned Men', 'For Both of You', 'Drayton Cemetery', 'The Wholly Innocent', 'Kind for Kind', 'Bimbo', 'Looking Down From Bridges', 'The Affair', 'Big Jim', 'Exiles', 'Nemesis', 'Around El Salvador', 'Revenants', 'Then', 'College Days', 'Beforehand', 'Planning a Service'.
2. Are Dawe's elegiac poems 'songs of light and darkness, affirmations of the spirit', as he said they were?
3. Is Dawe obsessed with melancholy and death?

Sympathy with 'bottom-dog'

1. 'Dawe never condemns anyone who is poor, out-of-work, or suffering hardships.' Is this true? ('The Flashing of Badges', 'The Family Man', 'The Victims', 'Drifters', 'One Jump Ahead', 'The Boy', 'Pleasant Sunday Afternoon'.)
2. Is Dawe a sympathetic but helpless bystander at the sorrows and tragedies he records? (Poems about war as well as the poems listed in the preceding question may be relevant.)
3. Consider Dawe's view of animals and their relation to human beings. ('Dogs in the Morning Light', 'Pigeons Also Are a Way of Life', 'The Hunter at Sunset', 'The Tree Pulled Down', 'The Frog Plague', *Gorilla gorilla*', 'Cattle at Night-Fall', 'The Bantams', 'Seeing Eye', 'Kind for Kind', 'Bimbo', 'The Ant-Lion', 'The Little Blokes', 'The Cough', 'Planning a Service'.)

Dramatic monologue

A poem in which a single speaker who is not the poet reveals something of his temperament, character, and history. The moment chosen for revelation is often a critical or characteristic one and there is often a sense of a specific audience listening and interacting.

1. 'Dawe's speakers in his dramatic monologues are all the same – hard-boiled, tough, and insensitive.' Is this true? ('And a Good Friday Was Had By All', 'The Not-So-Good Earth', A Victorian Hangman Tells His Love', 'Weapons Training', 'Pleasant Sunday Afternoon', 'The Vision Splendid', 'Little Dorrit Street', 'Uncle Arthur'.)

2. 'The speakers in Dawe's dramatic monologues are supposed to be ordinary people, but they are too eloquent to sustain this characterisation.' Do you think there is too much of Dawe's own linguistic brilliance in what his characters say?

Humour

1. Find one poem by Dawe that is entirely funny and another where humour is used to sharpen melancholy or sorrow. How does he move from one funny point to another? Contrast this with the way he moves from a funny point to a sorrowful one.
2. Do you prefer Dawe's humour when it arises from farcical situations or when it lies in his verbal wit?

Public quality

1. What evidence is there of concern for affairs of public interest in Dawe's work?
2. Is Dawe a preacher? Are his poems constructed for effective recitation in public?

Recent poems

1. What feelings does Dawe represent as appropriate for white Australians when they consider the Aborigines? ('Exiles', 'Beggars' Choice', 'Nemesis'.)
2. Is there any evidence of sentimentality in poems such as 'Seeing Eye', 'The Wholly Innocent', 'Grief', 'Bimbo', 'Big Jim', 'The Turnstiles', 'Definition of Loving', and 'Then'? How does Dawe try to neutralise or balance this tone?
3. What does Dawe have to say about ageing and feeling nostalgic or neglected? ('Drayton Cemetery', 'Looking Down From Bridges', 'Uncle Arthur', 'Then', 'Beforehand'.)
4. 'For Dawe the most prized aspect of love is endurance.' Is this true in 'With You Not By Me', 'A Peasant Idyll', 'Then', and 'Beforehand'?

Specimen answers

1. 'Humour...can be a very disarming form of seriousness.' Consider this statement by Dawe in relation to a few of his poems.

The number of Bruce Dawe's entirely humorous poems is quite small.

'Awkward Situation in Garden of Hesperides' is about a serious subject – the judgment of poetry – but is treated in an entirely light-hearted vein. 'Life-Cycle' has a similarly sustained set of humorous manoeuvres, but behind it all, glimpsed here and there in the language, is the sense that this excited activity and ritual are symbols for or a substitute for a religious attitude to life. 'Pleasant Sunday Afternoon' is more thoroughly farcical: as in 'Awkward Situation', the reader can enjoy the absurdity without worrying too much about whether the subject or the outcome of the episode deserve solemn consideration. By treating poetic judgment as a kind of alcoholic garden party and by using the figure of an encyclopaedia salesman (almost as automatic a figure of fun as the used-car salesman) Dawe has effectively stifled any hint of seriousness.

But such poems are rare. Even Dawe's confessedly 'light-verse' poems – those written for his weekly column in *The Toowoomba Chronicle* – often touch on matters of great moment. What look like humorous poems because of their surface texture and tone are often poems about critical moral principles. The humour is used to convey and illustrate the point and to make it memorable.

'Condolences of the Season', for instance, is not just a satire of feminine 'baby-worship'. It makes the point – reinforced by other poems by Dawe – that life is mainly filled with trivial incidents and that we are the victims of others' opinions of us. There is a touch of the mock-heroic about 'must suffer with like fortitude', for the list of what is to be endured is made up of minor irritations rather than genuine sufferings. It is, however, the cumulative effect of such irritations, the fact that they are inescapable throughout the whole of life, and the fact that life is not said to be made up of anything else that constitute genuine human suffering. Faced with a life like this, the best the human being can do is endure (Dawe always admires 'fortitude') and laugh (with a 'droll heretical wink').

'Credo' is more obviously a poem with serious implications. It has its patina of popular culture (Colonel Sanders, imitative advertising, mindless car driving) and its farcical interlude about the lost false teeth, but it is clearly centred on the nature of life and belief about life in Australia. These serious matters are conveyed through continued imagery of car-driving and eating. They are the images Dawe has chosen to represent the Australian attitude. They may be trivial, mindless and vulgar, but that is his point. Even the notion of what is beyond death can be represented by an expensive hotel or motel (recommended by one or more 'stars' in the guide book) where one carries on eating familiar items and seeing familiar scenes.

This poem makes a serious criticism of the lack of a spiritual dimension in Australian culture, but it depends for its substance and memorability on an outlook that is simultaneously humorous and earnest, a seriocomic vision. The approach of death is the approach of dark while driving on a country road. What is beyond is a star in the form of a starred hotel. But there are two differences in the analogy. The usually tender Australian steaks are now 'mysteriously leathery' (for what is beyond death will be both a mystery and something unexpected) and the celestial lamps are only 'almost' like those of earth. Here the point of view, though still humorously expressed, has gone beyond the limitations of the poet as a typical secular Australian to the slightly fearful insight of the poet as a person of spiritual perception.

COMMENT: The proposition posed in the question is not an easy one to demonstrate conclusively, but this answer might have been better had it been organised to show two or three specific ways in which humour disarms but then reinforces seriousness, for example, by making fun of a pompous person, by comic exaggeration, by farcical invention, and by punning. The answer nevertheless shows close acquaintance with serveral of Dawe's poems. Consideration of 'The Swimming Pool', 'In the Negative', 'The Affair', and 'Getting It Together' would also have been appropriate.

---

2. Do you think Dawe's style of political satire has changed? In your answer give close attention to one early and one late poem.

'Only the Beards are Different' and 'Around El Salvador' seem appropriate poems to compare. They were written twenty years apart (in 1961 and 1981) following political turmoil in Central America. 'Only the Beards Are Different' seems to have Dr Fidel Castro's 1959 revolution in Cuba as a major part of its background. In 1960 and 1961 there had also been changes in the dictatorial governments of El Salvador and the Dominican Republic. 'Around El Salvador' was written against a background of rapid changes of government juntas; military repression; persecution of priests, industrial workers, and peasants; widespread corruption; and economic mismanagement.

One other political comparison between Cuba in 1961 and El Salvador in 1981 is the inescapable interest of the United States – the chief of 'the mighty friends' – in the affairs of Central America. That interest is mentioned in 'Around El Salvador' but not in 'Only the Beards Are Different'. The reason probably goes beyond these particular poems. In the twenty years separating them Dawe has become more specific in the targets of his political satire. In 1961 he mentioned no country by name. Even the region is not mentioned; the poem could indeed, be applied equally aptly to the troubles in such newly independent African countries as the Belgian Congo, except that Castro's beard was so striking a part of his appearance and that he was widely regarded as the very model of a revolutionary. By 1981, Dawe's satires were usually more specific and noticeably more bitter. He seemed more enraged at injustice and oppression and more committed to exposing them. To be effective he had to identify the object more precisely, so that readers could not distance themselves from it or pretend that they were not implicated. Even the details are more specific and more vivid. In 'Only the Beards Are Different', for instance, executions are described in almost casual terms, the victims 'crumpling up/Against the sunpocked wall'. In 'Around El Salvador', the murder of Archbishop Romero and others is painfully vivid and brutal:

– Romero's blood runs down the altar steps,
the execution squads adorn the streets

That is not to say that the earlier political satires were not sometimes full of anger and compassion. 'Burial Ceremony', arising from the experiences of the Hungarian people in the years following Soviet intervention, is sufficient evidence on this point. But there are other early satires, like 'Everybody Sing', where the poet's attack reaches full force more slowly: the reader has to consider the implications of the comments before realising the thoroughgoing nature of the criticism being made. The language does not convey the urgent anger to be found in poems such as 'Around El Salvador'.

The major difference in the language between the early and the later political satires lies perhaps in the point of view. In the early ones, the revolution or counter-revolution has taken place. Nothing may have changed for the better, there may be an air of resignation; there is no eagerness or hope for another revolution, no feeling that the wrongs may yet be righted. In the later political satires, while there is no preaching of revolution, the political gloom has darkened to the point where cataclysm or apocalypse seems imminent. The point can be made by reference to the last line of each of the poems under review. 'Only the Beards Are Different' ends with 'Somewhere the country's saviour cries in his sleep'. The poem is so general that the reference works in three possible ways: to some past 'saviour' of the country, whose work has been obliterated; to some future 'saviour' yet to emerge; or, just conceivably, to the Saviour of the World. In 'Around El Salvador', the last line is 'The Saviour finds a Cross to stretch upon'. The reference has been taken away from politics and brought firmly into the moral and religious sphere. Here there may be – though it remains unstated in this poem – some room for hope. In other words, the earlier satires tend to finish in political quiescence; the later ones begin with more specific political references but end in moral and religious generalities. In a sense, Dawe has become gloomier politically, but more insistent on ultimate justice.

COMMENT: The argument is not as persuasive as it might have been if there had been more close attention to linguistic detail, such as there is at the end of the second paragraph. There might also have been some discussion of Dawe's support for the underdog, whether a person battered by society or a country oppressed by powerful neighbours. The reference to the early poems 'Burial Ceremony' and 'Everybody Sing' provides useful additional support for the point being made. (Did you notice the overtones of W.B. Yeats in 'Burial Ceremony'?) It is a pity that the argument about the later political satire was not reinforced by reference to another poem or two.

Part 5
Suggestions for further reading

The text

Sometimes Gladness: Collected Poems, 1954–1982, Longman Cheshire, Melbourne, 1983, is the most comprehensive edition of the poetry of Bruce Dawe. It substantially expands *Sometimes Gladness: Collected Poems, 1954–1978*, Longman Cheshire, Melbourne, 1978, not only by including a great many later poems but also by reprinting some earlier poems not found in the first edition. A still earlier collection, *Condolences of the Season: Selected Poems*, Cheshire, Melbourne, 1971, contains a few early poems omitted from the later volumes. The separate volumes from which the collections are mostly compiled are listed immediately below.

Other works by Dawe (chronologically)

No Fixed Address, Cheshire, Melbourne, 1962.
A Need of Similar Name, Cheshire, Melbourne, 1965.
An Eye for a Tooth, Cheshire, Melbourne, 1968.
Beyond the Subdivisions, Cheshire, Melbourne, 1969.
Heat-Wave, Sweeney Reed, Melbourne, 1970.
Bruce Dawe Reads From His Own Work (Poets on Record series: accompanied by 7-inch 45 rpm audiorecord), University of Queensland Press, St Lucia, 1971.
Dimensions, edited by Bruce Dawe, McGraw-Hill, Sydney, 1974.
Just a Dugong at Twilight: Mainly Light Verse, Cheshire, Melbourne, 1975.
'Australian Poets in Profile: 1', *Southerly*, 39, No. 3 (1979), 235–44.
Bruce Dawe Reads His Poems (audiocassette), Longman Cheshire, Melbourne, 1983.
'Public Voices and Private Feeling', in *The American Model: Influence and Independence in Australian Poetry*, edited by Joan Kirkby, Hale & Iremonger, Sydney, 1982, 160–72.
Over Here, Harv! and Other Stories, Penguin Books, Melbourne, 1983.

Critical studies

ASTLEY, T: 'The Shock of the Expected: Bruce Dawe's *Condolences of the Season*', in her *Three Australian Writers: Essays on Bruce Dawe, Barbara Baynton and Patrick White*, Townsville Foundation for Australian Literary Studies, Townsville, 1979, 1–11.

BENNETT, B. and DIBBLE, B,: 'An Interview with Bruce Dawe', *Westerly*, 24, No. 4 (1979), 63–84.

BROCK, P.: 'A View of Bruce Dawe's Poetry', *Southerly*, 42, No. 2 (1982), 226–37.

CARTER, D.: 'The Death of Satan and the Persistence of Romanticism', *Literary Criterion* (Mysore), 15, No. 3/4 (1980); also issued as *An Introduction to Australian Literature*, ed. C.D. Narasimhaiah, Wiley, Brisbane, 1982, 59–82 (72–7).

DIXON, J.: *Brodie's Notes on The Poetry of Bruce Dawe*, Pan, Sydney, 1981.

HAINSWORTH, J.: 'Paradoxes of Bruce Dawe's Poetry', *Southerly*, 36, No. 2 (1976), 186–93.

HANSEN, I.V. (ED.): *Bruce Dawe: The Man Down the Street*, Department of Education for the Victorian Association for the Teaching of English, Melbourne, 1972.

HEADON, D.: 'The Quick and the Dead: The Breadth of Australia's Poetry in the Last Decade', *Rocky Mountain Review of Language and Literature*, 32 (Spring 1978), 93–119.

LAW, P.: 'Raining Down Meaning: The Poetry of Bruce Dawe', *Southerly*, 39, No. 2 (1979), 192–203.

MCDONALD, R.: 'Bruce Dawe: An Interview with Roger McDonald', *Australian Writers on Tape*, University of Queensland Press, St Lucia, 1973.

MCGREGOR, C. and others: *In the Making*, Nelson, Melbourne, 1969.

MACLEOD, M.: 'Bruce Dawe and the Americans', *Australian Literary Studies*, 9 (1979) 143–55.

MARTIN, P.: 'In the Matter of Law v. Dawe: Case for the Defence', *Southerly*, 39, No. 4 (1979), 355–63.

SHAW, B.: *Times and Seasons: An Introduction to Bruce Dawe*, Cheshire, Melbourne, 1974.

WALLACE-CRABBE, C.: 'Bruce Dawe's Inventiveness', *Meanjin*, 35, No. 1 (1976), 94–101.

WRIGHT, J.M.: 'Bruce Dawe's Poetry', *Westerly*, 19, No. 1 (1974), 36–44.

The author of these notes

K.L. GOODWIN, educated at the University of Sydney and Balliol College, Oxford, is now Professor of English at the University of Queensland, Australia. His interest in Commonwealth Literature led to his election as chairman of the Association for Commonwealth Literature and Language Studies (1977–80). His publications include *The Influence of Ezra Pound; National Identity* (ed.); *Commonwealth Literature in the Curriculum* (ed.); and *Understanding African Poetry* (1982).